Business Experts React t

THE DEATH OF 20ᵗʰ CENTURY SELLING ...

"Funny, unforgettable, and totally unique. Want your sales to come alive? Read this book! A powerful collection of sales war stories and water cooler wisdom, it's packed with the hard-earned lessons of grizzled sales veterans. A must for your sales arsenal!"
— Chris J. Witting, *Success Journal Radio Network*

"We can learn valuable lessons from the experience of others. Dan's collection of sales horror stories can help both the new and experienced salesperson avoid dangerous pitfalls. I encourage you to read the stories and apply the lessons you learn."
— Peter Handal, President & CEO Dale Carnegie Training

"Dan Seidman provides the sugar that helps the medicine go down in the form of humor that enlightens as it tickles."
— Jay Conrad Levinson, author, *Guerrilla Marketing* series of books

"Here is a powerful presentation of material to make you cringe, cry and of course, laugh. BUT, pay attention to the real reason this book was written - you may be antagonizing prospects with obsolete selling strategies. If you value your business and want an entertaining presentation, have Dan talk to your people. He'll save you money while he makes you laugh. You won't regret it!"
— Raleigh Pinskey, author, *101 Ways to Promote Yourself*

"This book proves that nobody is totally useless. They can always be used as a bad example. Dan Seidman is the best example of a 180-degree U-turn in selling strategy in the world—he brings the dead (sales) back to life."
— Jeffrey Gitomer, author, *The Sales Bible*

"Dan Seidman finds the 'teachable moments' in the blunders of these sales klutzes and barbarians—and the rest of us get a roll-on-the-floor belly laugh! My favorite was the story of the clown who shoplifted from his prospect, and got caught."

— Shel Horowitz, author,
Grassroots Marketing: Getting Noticed in a Noisy World

"Here's the first book that educates people on what *no longer* works, and does it with real examples that also happen to be very funny. This book leads you to sales success—and offers you a few laughs along the way."

— Rieva Lesonsky, Editorial Director, *Entrepreneur Magazine*

"Often, we learn best from the mistakes of other people – and these lessons stay with us longer. This book is a creative, enjoyable, non-traditional look at what has ot worked in the lives of other sales reps."

— The Sandler Sales Institute

"Stories so funny they have to be true! And that's why they're so useful—must reading for anyone who sells for a living (or wants to)."

— Seth Godin, *Unleashing the Ideavirus*

"This is great stuff! Some people are funny and some people are terrific sales trainers. You're the first person I have met who is a truly funny and impactful sales trainer. There's no better tonic than the occasional shot of humility. Anyone who has ever sold anything has been there. From reading this I had a great laugh, a chance to poke fun at myself as a sales person and I learned a ton. Thank you."

— Donald A. Connelly, Senior Marketing Officer,
Putnam Retail Management

"Here's what I learned: You can fool some of the people all of the time and all of the people some of the time, just make sure none of these people are your customers."

— Joe Himelfarb, Hewlett Packard

"This is a rare book. Not only does it teach you what not to do, it delivers the lesson in such a way that you can die laughing. I spit all over my computer screen when I read one of the stories. The last time I laughed this hard was when I was a kid and milk came out my nose. I love this book. Devour it and it will help you make more money while keeping you from making a fool of yourself. Learn from Dan. He's the man."

—Joe Vitale, author of way too many book to list, including
There's A Customer Born Every Minute

"This is a great book of incredible sales experiences. I loved it!"
— Brian Tracy, Author, Speaker, Consultant

"A chance to laugh and learn at the same time."
— Paul & Sarah Edwards, authors, *Getting Business to Come to You*

"Seidman's approach is refreshing. For too long, the how-to bakery of sales prospecting has been hawking day-old bread."
— Pete Miller, VP Sales, LC Thomsen

"When I read your story about the coconuts, my thoughts were, 'and I thought I was one hell of a salesman. Here's a real master.'"
— Gunjan Saraf, *WorkingHumor.com*

"After reading this book, every sales manager will ask a few more questions about the prospects that never became customers. There may be more to the story of the troubled customer who seems indecisive. He may have been scared off by a Sales Dinosaur!"
— Sam Reese, President, *Miller Heiman Sales Training*

"Highly entertaining reading — with practical, immediately useable wisdom—sets this book apart from the herd of sales literature. If you sell anything, or aspire to, it's a must read!"
— Marilyn Ross, speaker, consultant, author,
Shameless Marketing for Brazen Hussies

The Death
of 20th Century
Selling

50 Hilarious Sales Blunders and
How You can Profit from Them

Dan Seidman

**SALES
AUTOPSY**

PRESS

THE DEATH OF 20TH CENTURY SELLING
50 Hilarious Sales Blunders and How You can Profit from Them

Sales Autopsy Press
190 E. Dundee Rd.
Barrington IL USA 60010
www.SalesAutopsy.com

To order the book, contact your local bookstore or call 1-877-613-7355

Credits
Manuscript Evaluation Gordon Burgett
Editing Joe Shaw
Text Design/ Production Michael Brechner
Graphics Wizard Ken Seidman
Cover Design Jim Weems, Ad Graphics, Inc.
Cover Model Dan Seidman

Library of Congress Cataloging-in-Publication Data
Seidman, Dan.
   The death of twentieth-century selling : 50 hilarious sales blunders and how you can profit from them / by Dan Seidman.
          — 1ˢᵗ ed.
          p. cm.
          Death of 20th century selling
          Includes index.
          LCCN 2001118661
          ISBN 0-9712911-0-1
          1. Selling. 2. Sales personnel – Anecdotes.
   I. Title. II. Title: Death of 20th century selling

   HF5438.25.S45 2002   658.85
                                         QBI01-201185

First printing 2002

          2   4   6   8   9   7   5   3   1

About the Author

DAN SEIDMAN HAS BEEN INVOLVED in high-impact sales and marketing for privately run companies since 1980. He is an early adopter of the Internet, selling for the first Internet job site, Online Career Center in 1993. Dan took his extensive sales management and training expertise online in '99. He currently manages the widely publicized website of selling disasters, SalesAutopsy.com. *Sales & Marketing Management Magazine* calls the site "a cult hit among sales folks."

The website has garnered massive amounts of publicity over the last two years. This has led to international recognition in the sales and marketing community. His sales stories have been featured in business publications and trade magazines worldwide.

Dan invests his business life in speaking to entrepreneurs, sales professionals and executives about these amusing, lesson-filled sales horror stories.

On the personal side, Dan enjoys scuba diving and competes in World Master's Sports, where he is a two-time gold medallist in basketball, playing on a United States team.

He also volunteers on the Web advisory board for Willow Creek Association, the board of Sales and Marketing Executives of Chicago and serves as the ezine editor for the Small Publishers Association of North America.

He lives in Inverness, Illinois with his precious wife, Wendy and their near-perfect son, Joshua. Twin girls were recently discovered at his residence; they're being referred to as Abigail and Rebekah. Contact Dan by e-mail at dan@SalesAutopsy.com.

Preface

On the Psychology of a Book that Focuses on Selling Stupidly as Opposed to Selling Successfully

THE LATE, GREAT SALES GENIUS, David Sandler, used to tell a story of a boy who went to an action movie to watch people getting into trouble, falling into quicksand, being attacked, and having other exciting, dangerous experiences. The little boy loved to see others in misery, Sandler explained. After all, it's tough being a little kid.

So, the question I asked the sales world was this: Do people prefer hearing about successes or failures? Super successes can be inspiring, but can reflect our own lack of them, leaving us a bit empty after the inspiration wears off. Failure can be funny and a relief: "Thank God that didn't happen to me." And the tales of sales that failed are much more fun to share with colleagues and friends. Few people laugh at success, but everyone laughs at stark raving failure. I'd rather you laugh long and hard at someone's misery than be momentarily moved by his or her success.

Bottom line? We sales professionals and entrepreneurs are just like that little kid. After all, it's tough being a sales professional. Let's laugh and learn from our fellow reps. Laughter is cleansing and healing. Laughter is my gift to you, the reader of these stories.

Thanks for reading this book and making me a part of your journey to the highest levels of selling success. Enjoy the ride!

Dan Seidman, Inverness, Illinois

Foreword

In 1835, Samuel Haliburton wrote a number of stories about an imaginary salesman named Sam Slick who traveled through Connecticut selling clocks. The purpose of the series of articles was to incite his readers to become more enterprising. Haliburton minted memorable quotes that millions of people use today without remembering their creator. He came up with sayings like "Six of one or half a dozen of the other," "Barking up the wrong tree," and "Failures to heroic minds are the stepping stones to success."

Stories contain the seeds that fuel our ambition. When someone tells us a story, we listen to the kernel of truth, to the flash of insight or the lightning bolt of inspiration. Stories move us forward to grab the brass ring, and they help us avoid the pitfalls that wipe others out.

While stories about success may fill readers with awe or envy, they often fail to motivate those who lack self-esteem. Stories about failures have a dual benefit: First, failures or fumbles are entertaining to read. Second, failures are wonderful teachers who often bring out the best in us. Seidman has collected some of the best failure stories, which work like strong vitamins that boost our immune system so we can protect ourselves against adversity, rejection, or defeat.

Remember the old saying, "When the student is ready, the teacher will appear." Dan Seidman is the teacher who allows the sales professional to enjoy the drama of a sales situation. He then illuminates the mind of the reader with keen insights, useful advice, and practical suggestions. These stories are all written from the heart. In a high-tech age filled with confusion, this collection of real-life stories appears as a breath of fresh air.

This book is not a cure for blunders. On the contrary, the main message of the book is to encourage you as a salesperson to fail forward. It's a lot more realistic than to get stuck in one place and pretend to be growing. The moral of every story in this book is very simple: If we don't learn to fail, we'll never learn to grow.

Gerhard Gschwandtner
Publisher, *Selling Power Magazine*

Acknowledgments

I COULDN'T HAVE DONE IT WITHOUT...

◆ All of you who had the guts to confess your sales blunders

◆ The best parents a guy could pick out of a lineup. I love you mom and dad!

◆ Three brothers who, with me, have yet to confess some hilarious horror stories to our parents

◆ Bill Bartlett of Corporate Strategies, Illinois who cheered, encouraged and laughed with me when I left training to follow this dream

◆ Jeffrey Gitomer who needs to get into your face too, and make you a better sales professional and person

◆ Dan Poynter who set me on the publishing path at light-year speed and with the wisdom of Yoda

◆ Tad Ballantyne, Rich Childs and Dennis Mutch for decades of laughter, friendship and financial success

◆ Dr. Edward deBono for amazing inspiration in creative thinking

◆ Wendy's parents who are so cool we actually vacation with them!

And many, many thanks to my guest gurus who graciously gave me content that supports the stories and learning contained in this book:
Dale Dauten, the Corporate Curmudgeon
Robert Dilts, world-class NLP and leadership trainer
Jeffrey Fox, Rainmaker
Dave Kurlan, salesforce assessment expert
Dr. Ivan Misner, found of Business Network International
Tom Sant, sales proposal software expert
Joe Sugarman, Mr. BluBlocker
Roy H. Williams, the Wizard of Ads

And This Book Is Dedicated to...

WELL, THIS BABY COULD NOT HAVE BEEN BIRTHED without the encouragement and love of my precious wife Wendy and the three she gave birth to – Joshua, Abigail and Rebekah. This family nourishes my heart, soul and laugh muscles.

Introduction

Who done it?
A sales murder mystery!

HAVE YOU EVER had a sale die? Have you ever lost a sale because you killed it? What lesson did you learn? Or did you just grumble and blame others.

In my thirty years of sales training and consulting I've never had a salesperson come up to me and say, "Jeffrey, I didn't make the sale, and it was all my fault!" Salespeople always blame the death of their sales on things like lower prices, better relationship with someone else, pre-existing contracts, unreturned phone calls — you know the drill — anything and anyone but the face they see in the morning bathroom mirror.

Salespeople are always studying sales looking for the best (or easiest) way to make a sale. But they don't seem to really learn unless they hit a brick wall. That pain sinks in.

When I began reading these sales horror stories through Dan's ezine, I laughed and learned from each one. But as I read the book, I realized that here was a collection of sales coal turned into sales diamonds. For the first time in sales history, someone has taken the horror of sales and not only humanized the response, but created a mouth-to-mouth form of "selling resuscitation."

This isn't a book about lost sales. No, no. This is a book about how you can learn to win sales by not making the same mistakes of others. This isn't a book about other people's blunders. This is a book about how you can make more sales by gaining insight (the cause of death after each story) about other salespeople's sales mistakes, so you don't have to make them yourself.

13

Vicarious learning:
You see the pain, but don't actually feel it.

WHEN YOU READ ABOUT other people's sales death, you chuckle at the story, the circumstance, and the stupidity. It also allows you to "Monday-morning quarterback" about how you would have *never* done that. But the *real value* in these autopsies is the prevention of *your lost sales*. Because in the end, that's what you really care about.

So let me give you some major clues about how to use this book to save sales, save face, save customers, save dollars, and save your career.

The stories are ingeniously grouped by the "type" of failure so that you can see how deaths take place by person *and* personality. Old techniques, bad attitude, too much ego or anger, a poor system for selling, or — my favorite — the "go figure" sales death that plagues us all.

Each story tells of the death of a sale in the words of the person who killed it. Classic miscues, poor judgments, and boners that they committed and then were brave enough to fess up what *really* happened. These salespeople are to be commended.

After each story, Dan presents a postmortem to determine the cause of death. Like an autopsy performed by a pathologist, Dan leads you to an understanding of why this death occurred. And those "why" lessons are designed to prevent your sales death.

Between the lessons, Dan also takes the time to share his own sales concepts and philosophies, a perfect blend of information about the reality between old and new perspectives of selling.

As a rule, I don't read current books on selling. It ruins my independent thought and creativity as a writer and speaker. I read the sales classic literature written fifty years ago or more. These books can only be found in used bookstores, and even though they're much less expensive than the shiny new ones, they contain the history and the philosophy of selling at its purest, and sales "answers" at their finest. They tell the way sales should be made — and in fact, the easiest way to sell. The rare title, *How to Sell Your Way Through Life,* written by Napoleon Hill in the late twenties and early thirties, remains the best book ever written on the subject.

But when I read *The Death of 20ᵗʰ Century Selling* I was taken aback. This book is both a throwback and a leap forward. It embraces the concepts of yesterday, which rely more on the relationship and less on the hoodwinking, and it leaps forward with the progressive thoughts and insights necessary for 21st-century sales dominance — both individual and corporate. It is real-world examples and street-smart insights about how to make bad situations good.

Salespeople have been dying since Henry Miller wrote *Death of a Salesman* fifty years ago, but the rebirth of the selling process is alive and in your hands.

Dan Seidman has created the best example of a 180-degree U-turn in selling strategy I've ever read — he brings the dead (sales) back to life.

But here's the secret to this book and your success. The best way to read, enjoy, *and* benefit from this book is to "sip" it. Read the stories one at a time, one each day. After you read it, put the lesson into action the same day. If you read it, and study it, and apply the principles in it, and put the lessons into *your* sales actions, at the end of sixty days you'll be on the sales path to success. *Healed!*

With the proper self-discipline, you can convert the death of *The Death of 20th Century Selling* into living sales and eternal relationships.

I hope you do.

Jeffrey Gitomer
Author of *The Sales Bible,*
Customer Satisfaction is Worthless,
Customer Loyalty is Priceless,
Knock Your Socks Off Selling,
YES! A Wonderful Alternative to N

How This Book Came into Existence

WHAT'S THE BLUEPRINT for this book? That is the question we asked as we looked for a structure into which we would build these pages. The stories themselves gave us the answer. We selected the top hundred selling blunders and identified the basic reason for each failure. We then storyboarded the tales on a chart and found that a pattern emerged. The failures fell into four basic categories: salespeople failed because they used old techniques, exhibited a bad attitude (often because they were rookies), let their egos (or anger) control them, or employed an ineffective selling system. For each category, we assigned a name to the sales character it represented.

Thus birth was given to the Sales Dinosaur, Tourist, Napoleon, and Maverick. Each story has a "postmortem" or autopsy to review what killed the sale, just as a doctor would dissect a body to discover what ended a life. Fortunately, you will also receive suggestions about how to fix each trouble (often with a unique strategy), avoid the mistakes of others, and shorten your learning curve to selling success.

I've also added a category called Miscellaneous Malpractice, because every now and then weird things happen over which we have no control. These are my favorites, the funniest stories.

The Death of 20th Century Selling is a sad but accurate choice of title. It refers to the fact that each of these sales characters is a reflection of changes we should seriously consider.

Ninety-nine percent of the sales professionals, managers, and entrepreneurs I talk to are dissatisfied with the quality of their prospects, frustrated by their interaction with those prospects, and unhappy with the amount of money they take home.

The good news is that new, highly effective techniques do exist. New assessment tools can identify a rookie's chances for success, and superb selling systems can make a sales professional's life much easier and much more profitable.

Who needs to read this book?

Anyone who is in sales, used to be in sales, knows a salesperson, or has butted heads with a salesperson
You'll get some great laughs and pick up a few tips along the way. Everyone loves someone who shares a funny story. Here's a "greatest hits from the past" collection to enjoy.

Salespeople and entrepreneurs who had training long ago or never received any
Many of your techniques don't work like they used to (maybe they never worked that well at all!). With each story, you get a lesson learned that includes what strategies work better today.

Trainers, teachers, and managers who need some funny, true tales to prove their points
Your training sessions, classrooms, and sales meetings will be much more lively and memorable if you build humor into your teaching. A dose of reality is a powerful learning tool.

Here's the bottom line for selling success: Find a system, learn it, and use it. You'll see the value of that belief revealed throughout the stories. Let's get right to the fun.

And we're off and stumbling ...

Contents

The Death
of 20th Century
Selling

Sales Dinosaur

Part One
Sales Dinosaur

LET'S BEGIN THIS JOURNEY into the death of twentieth-century selling by looking at the character who is probably part of the genetic sales structure of all of us.

The Sales Dinosaur is using outdated techniques that are no longer effective. You can identify this lumbering beast as it crushes buyers in three ways:

It uses manipulative questions and tactics
It does most of the talking in a sales call
It sounds like every other salesperson out there (boring!)

This sales animal will soon be extinct. Many older sales approaches that were effective in the 70s, 80s and 90s are no longer useful. How is this true? Buyers are better at buying than sellers are at selling. Memorize that statement, because you'll realize its truth when you look into the eyes of a prospect as you respond to a "closing" question with a snappy response. That prospect knows what strategy you're attempting. (Once the prospect is aware of the tactic, it becomes nothing more than a trick — and nobody wants to be tricked.)

Buyers are better at buying for three reasons. First, they've heard all of those closes. Salespeople have been hounding them all day long for years. They probably know most closes better than we do. Secondly, there's so much information available (thank you, *Consumer Reports*, trade magazines, and, of course, the Worldwide Web). Prospects are researching you and your competition long before they sit down with you. Thirdly, we as salespeople have spent many years training buyers how to act. We've led them to expect loads of information. We've taught them that if they ask our price up-front, they get it, because we don't want to offend them. We've led them to believe that their time is more valuable than ours is, so we have to beg for appointments. The real result of these horrible old practices is impotent salespeople. You need an edge. You need to be different. You need to act differently than every other salesperson out there.

Foot in Mouth Kills Salesman in Front of Client

Rick shares how he choked on his chance for a big sale

I SELL PRINTING SERVICES in Chicago. And I'm probably not as good as I am persistent. It took six months of phone calls and mailed literature to finally get into the president's office of a company that I wanted to sell very badly. It took less than thirty seconds to undo half a year of time and effort.

I'd finally nailed this guy down to an appointment and wanted to make a really good first impression. I figured that this president would look at me as either a strong, persistent salesman or a pest. He would dispose of a pest as quickly as he could, so as I walked into his office, I looked for something on the wall or on his desk that I could use for a little opening small talk.

"John Madden!" I cried, pointing at an 8 10 photograph on his credenza. Every sports fan knows the 300-plus-pound commentator. He's probably the best announcer around, in spite of an ugly mug that could stop a bus. "How did you get a photograph of yourself with your arm around John Madden?"

My rapport-building efforts crashed in flames as the shocked company president slowly answered, "That's not John Madden, that's … my … wife."

POSTMORTEM

OUR POOR SALESMAN, RICK, used an approach that was popular early in the evolution of selling. Are you like this at the initial contact with a prospect? Do you look for that fish on the wall, the trophy on the shelf, the picture on the desk? We're often taught to comment on these items to "break the ice." Can you distinguish yourself by being so ordinary? Don't sound like everyone else who sells. This small talk is wasteful and disrespectful of a buyer's time. Here's a suggestion for that initial contact that many top-performing sales pros use today: Recognize that your prospects don't have the time to chat like they used to. Simply respect the prospect's time, and review what you agreed upon when you got the appointment. Rick should have said, "Mr. Prospect, I want to respect your commitment to the time we have. When we talked on the phone you said we'd have forty-five minutes to talk. Is that right? Good. What is the most serious reason you felt it was important to invite me in today?" As a sales pro, you've now honored someone's busy schedule and gotten right to business. Best of all, the prospect is about to do most of the talking.

Enough to Make
A Grown Man Cry

*Dan the headhunter explains
his blown shot at a big fee*

**(Yes, this is Dan, your confessing author,
sharing a tale from my Sales Dinosaur days.)**

"I LOST MY REP ON THE SOUTH SIDE of Chicago," the medical products sales manager told me on the phone. He asked me to meet him at a tradeshow to discuss using my search skills to fill the position. My search fee would be about $12,000. I was really glad to meet at a tradeshow, since I could walk around and try to get more business from other companies exhibiting there.

The manager wasn't at the booth, but three of his reps were — two women, and a guy about twenty-four years old. "I'm here to meet John," I told them. They asked what I did and I made one of the dumbest mistakes of my career. "Oh, I'm a medical sales recruiter, and John wants me to help find a rep for the Chicago South territory." Dead silence, shocked looks, and suddenly the guy burst into tears, ran about twenty feet away, and started bawling.

"That's his territory," one of the women said. "He had no idea he was being replaced, or he didn't until now." I felt my heart plunge to the bottom of my belly. The manager had said the territory was open and the rep was gone. I tried to apologize to the guy, explaining my lack of information about him. He was cool, but he left the show, and wasn't at the booth a few minutes later when the manager arrived.

The manager was furious! Of course it was all my fault. He wanted me to find the replacement — for free. I left there completely disgusted with myself and without a signed contract. When that manager later called my office to ask my boss to make me work for free, my boss told him where to go. Then I had to explain the whole story to

28

my boss. I learned that all those sales books and tapes that tell you to promote yourself every chance you get are sometimes wrong.

 ## POSTMORTEM

WHAT A HORRIBLE EXPERIENCE for the young salesman and for me. Why do we always feel like we need to be talking? I suggest you keep your mouth shut until you're in front of the decision-maker. If you want to make small talk, fine. But why try to resell yourself to everyone you meet? Your appointment with the decision-maker is already secured. If others ask who you are, simply say that you're an industry service provider who's been asked to sit down with your boss. Then get on another topic. Don't be a dinosaur, an old-fashioned salesperson who feels the need to talk much too much.

Automobile Fits Couple's Hearts, but Not Their Home

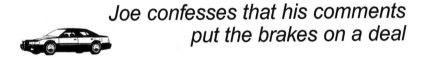

Joe confesses that his comments put the brakes on a deal

I was working an elderly couple who were buying a new Cadillac. They were looking forward to their first luxury car.

They drove a beautiful blue Coupe DeVille and just fell in love with it. This was probably the easiest sale I had ever made. We were 80 percent done with the paperwork, but no sale is legally binding until the taillights cross the driveway. So, while we're finishing up, I'm making small talk and keeping up the reinforcement that they'd made a great decision.

I said, "This car will sure look great in your driveway!"

"Oh, we have a garage." They replied.

"Well, you may want to leave it out to show your neighbors."
The lady turned to her husband and said, "Dear, do you think this

will fit in the garage?"

Now we had to check out their garage. I pretty much knew as I was driving there that, since there is a God in Heaven with a sense of humor, the car wouldn't fit, so I spent that time mentally kicking myself.

When we arrived, God had His laugh, and there went my sale!

POSTMORTEM

JOE'S LESSON IS ONE you'll want to take to heart. Once the prospect says yes, be silent. Comment only on conversation that new client initiates. I once kicked one of my sales reps in the ankle beneath the table for yapping after her prospect had already said yes. Her lesson came at the price of a pair of nylons. So be silent after the close, while your heart does all the cheering. When this story first came out, my postmortem was blasted by auto sales reps, who were angry because I didn't say that the salesperson should always do right by the customer, even if it means missing a sale. I stand corrected (even Dear Abby gets straightened out at times), and encourage you to deal with trouble when it arises. If I were Joe, I would have gotten a commitment to check out other vehicles if the garage was too small, and *then* head over to the couple's home.

Buyer Bites Head Off Rep

Melissa is maligned, she claims, by an experienced prospect

I WAS CALLING ON THE VICE PRESIDENT of human resources of a large company. The size of the account would easily have been the most significant insurance sale of my career.

The buyer was a soft-spoken older gentleman. I gently asked under what circumstances the prospect might move his firm's business to our company.

"Do you think you can beat our current insurance provider's pricing?" he asked.

"If we give you a better deal," I replied "would you be prepared to give us your business upon the presentation of my quote?"

The quiet prospect turned red in a flash of genuine anger. He pointed a long, stiff finger at me and spat out, "Young woman, if you ever use another closing technique on me, I will throw you out of this office. Do you understand? I'm sick of all you salespeople and your tricks."

I was so rattled that I never did save that sales call. The last ten minutes of the meeting were spoken in stiff, formal terms. I did the proposal, but never could get the VP on the phone again.

I learned that some of those techniques you learn to hook the buyer can backfire badly.

POSTMORTEM

MELISSA FELT TERRIBLE. She was a winner when she had actually landed an appointment with a very high-level decision-maker. Then she blew her shot at a big sale. Do you recognize the name of the closing technique that ruined her meeting? It's an oldie called "The Porcupine Close." If someone asks you a "closing" question, you turn it around and stick them with a question that demands a commitment to buy. Here, he asked if she could beat current pricing, and she stuck him with a request for a contract if she could beat the price. This outdated sales ploy was popular from the 1970s to the 1990s. Today, many buyers like that VP have heard so many closes that they know them as well as we do. Some are even angered by these attempts to pressure or manipulate. The lessons that follow this story will help you avoid this technique, and teach you to dig deeper and learn more about your prospect's real needs.

Never Say That!

Three Closes That Will Sink Your Ship Before It Sales

Thoughts on the Sales Dinosaur

AT WWW.SALESAUTOPSY.COM we collect stories of selling disasters. Many of these crash-and-burn experiences happen when salespeople practice useless old Dinosaur closing techniques.

You recall our revealing that buyers are better at buying than most salespeople are at selling. This means that if you continue to use old techniques, you run the risk of seriously annoying buyers. Here are three sales tales that show why the tactics used below need to be relegated to the elephant's graveyard of selling.

And there's hope: each sad story has a simple remedy.

1. The Impending Event Close

I (Dan, your war correspondent of selling) had just finished test driving a beautiful new car, and now sat across from an anxious salesperson. And thank God that I was the buyer for a change:

Salesperson: It's a great car, isn't it?
Dan: Yes.

Salesperson: You like that gold color?"

Dan: Yes.

Salesperson: We call it "pebble beige."

Dan: Oh.

Salesperson: It's our most popular color. In fact, that's only one of the reasons you'll want to place a deposit on the car today — because it won't be here tomorrow.

Dan: (slowly): That's the "impending event" close.

Salesperson: What's that you said?

Dan: You know. The "impending event close." If I don't decide to buy from you *right now,* a change in events will prevent me from buying later.

Salesperson: Uh, yeah, impending event … Say, what do you do for a living?

You recognize this selling ploy. It's an attempt to pressure the prospect to buy immediately. It's the old limited-time offer. You've probably experienced this trick with phone salespeople: "This proposal is only good until midnight tonight." The retail world thrives on this strategy. Want proof? Just look at your Sunday paper for the big, bold black-and-red letters screaming, "3 Days Only!" or "50% Off Today!" (See Roy Williams's article on Expiration-dated Advertising, page 44.)

The dumb question, of course, is whether there will be a sale tomorrow or next week. Of course there will be. There always is. So this selling strategy can be quite risky. Does the prospect really believe that there are no other choices out there beyond your product? Realize that if you, as a sales professional, make a statement that's not true (and the speculative "it won't be here tomorrow" falls into that category), you can have an angry, disbelieving, and disgusted prospect. Whether is shows on your buyer's face or not, if the prospect detects that you're lying or tricking him or her into a fast decision, you're dead — there will be no deal. Don't manipulate the truth to suit your desire to close the sale. Don't employ this very obvious sales trick.

Here's how you can cancel and replace that impending event close: Trim that bad language off your tongue like a WeightWatchers success story. Let's look at a before and after snapshot of word choices.

Before:

> *Salesperson:* That is our most popular color. In fact, that's only one of the reasons you'll want to place a deposit on the car today — because it won't be here tomorrow.

Rather than antagonize someone this way, replace the statement with a question like this:

After:

> *Salesperson:* "Mr. Prospect, I'm assuming that you probably don't want this exact model. Is that true?"

> *Prospect:* "What do you mean?"

> *Salesperson:* "Well, would it matter to you if it's gone next week?"

We're about to stumble upon a fork in the conversation. The prospect will either say, "I'll worry about that then." You just discovered that this person doesn't have an urgent need or you didn't create urgency to buy (that is, to solve his or her problem), or the prospect will say, "Can't you get another one just like it?" You just found out that the prospect is focused on getting what he or she wants.

Either way, you've allowed the buyer to determine the consequences of delayed action. He or she has put into words what you can only guess at. This creates a more professional conversation. You preserve that respect that is difficult to generate — and keep — by avoiding the temptation to mind-read the prospect with the risky "impending event" sales technique.

Here's the key: If you want to make an important statement, form it as a question that directs the prospect down the path you've chosen for him or her. You'll make more money by letting the buyer come to your conclusion, believing it's his or her own.

Trim the fat and lose the "impending event close" today.

2. The Porcupine Close

The buyer was genuinely interested in acquiring a new cell phone with a less expensive service contract.

Salesperson: It's a nice cell phone, isn't it?

Bill: Yes. I really like the voice-activated dialing.

Salesperson: So are you ready to take it home right now?

Bill: Well, I do want to know some details on the service contract. You know — monthly fees and all that. My old service is very expensive.

Salesperson: Bill, if we can beat the cost of your old plan, are you willing to sign with us right now?

Bill: (suddenly changing from friendly to icy) I think I'll check out some other options first.

Salesperson: Oh, sure. I understand. Let me give you some literature and my card.

Here's our old friend, the porcupine close. This archaic technique is based on an old sales training maxim: any question a prospect asks is a closing question — it expresses interest. So the porcupine turns around and sticks the prospect with his own question. This is supposed to work, because (traditionally) you are *never* to answer a question, you are to ask one in return. However, responding to a simple information request with a question that prematurely forces a buying decision can be a very delicate move.

Here's what you can do today to avoid getting stuck by the porcupine close:

Pushing to close a deal prematurely can only endanger the buyer/ seller relationship. It's much safer to let our prospect, Bill, expand on his desire for a less expensive cell phone by asking a simple open-ended question, not a closing question. Let's look at how differently the conversation evolves in our before-and-after scenarios.

Before:

Bill: Well, I do want to know some details on the service contract. You know monthly fees and all that. My old service is very expensive.

Salesperson: Bill, if we can beat the cost of your old plan, are you willing to sign with us right now?

After:

Salesperson: Expensive? Really? Is there something about the old plan ... ? (If you act slightly confused, the buyer will jump in to help.)

Bill: Sure, long distance isn't included. (or) I have a friend with a competing service who pays way less than I do.

Salesperson: Oh, so you use long distance a great deal? (or) You're probably looking at your friend's cell phone company as well, right?

Either way, you've discovered more information that will help you sell to the *exact needs* of that prospect. You haven't put premature pressure on this person by forcing a buying decision for which you would most likely get a stall or a no. Drop the porcupine close now and you won't get stuck in a similar selling scenario.

3. Why you should never ask why

Jennifer has just spent two hours attempting to sell a software program to a vice president of sales. She has shown every piece of marketing literature she carries. She has answered every question the man asked. It is showdown time.

VP of Sales: Well, I just don't think we are prepared to make a decision today. (The man flashes a courtesy smile and shakes his head)

Jennifer: (referring to an earlier benefit) Why wouldn't you be interested in reducing your sales team's prospecting time by forty percent?

The smile freezes on the VP's face, and his eyes narrow with Clint Eastwood-like intensity. Jennifer realizes that she won't be celebrating a big sale over a steak dinner tonight.

What just happened?

Jennifer has made a Tyrannosaurus-sized mistake. She is angry inside. Her stomach acid is increasing. After all, hasn't she just invested two hours in educating the prospect about her product? But she forces a smile and responds, according to her training, with a

36

"why" question. Jennifer just put the final nail in her commission coffin by choosing one wrong word. When she threw the word *why* into that sentence, she questioned the decision-making ability of that decision-maker. *Why* implies that he is stupid.

Think about it. She just gave him thirty-seven great reasons to buy and he said no. The question she really asked him was; "Are you stupid after hearing all of that, could you tell me *why* wouldn't you be interested in reducing your sales team's prospecting time by forty percent?"

This little, .22-caliber word is a silenced bullet
to the head of the person hearing it.

Why rarely works because, after using it and getting stonewalled, Jennifer will most likely backpedal and defend the greatness of her product, getting argumentative and in essence begging for the business. All because she chose to toss out *why* in a question.

Would you like to learn the reasons Jennifer and *you* do this all the time? Because you can bet your granddaddy's farm that tens of thousands of salespeople throw the word *why* at prospects every day.

This little .22-caliber word is a silenced bullet to the head of the person hearing it. Here's how that occurs:

Take a time-out for some time travel. You're sixteen years old and have just announced to your parents that you're going to try cliff diving with some friends. Dad looks at you and says, "*Why* in the world would you do that? That's unbelievably dumb, what a stupid decision, did I raise an idiot? Blah, blah, blah." Do you recall having a parent or other adult talk to you like that? Do you think it's a smart move to throw the prospect's unconscious mind back to that time when he or she was verbally beaten up for a choice they made?

Back to the present: Does it make sense that this simple word can be an extremely risky selection? To use language like that, to question the intelligence of a potential buyer, is simply foolish. You are implying that your solution is so good, so obvious, that only a fool would pass it up.

Thanks for identifying that pothole in my path to sales success, you're thinking. But what do I do instead of asking *why*?

Here's your strategy for removing *why* from your selling vocabulary:

First, realize that a *why* question can be answered quite briefly. This answer is probably in the form of an objection. To respond to this objection, you'll create an environment that is argumentative. Switch one simple word and you end up with an open-ended question that will draw some incredibly useful information from the prospect.

That word is *how*.

Let's put our new word to work on this buyer's stall tactic:

VP of Sales: Well, I just don't think we are prepared to make a decision today. (The man flashes a stiff smile and shakes his head.)

Jennifer: "Oh, *how* did you determine that we're not right, at this time, for you?"

Using *how* discards the "in your face" indictment of the prospect. Using *how* turns the question into a request for the *process* that a buyer has gone through to reach his or her decision. Understanding this concept is worth the weight of this book in gold.

Pay very close attention to the psychology of how this works. You want to draw out of the buyer a process or path the buyer traveled to get to a decision. *How* will help you unpack the buyer's brain and discover how that individual makes up his or her mind.

This is all about processes. And there are always two processes at work in a sale: An external process is the company's way of dealing with the review and potential purchase of products or services; an internal process is the individual decision-maker's way of determining that he or she will buy.

External Processes

If you've sold large accounts, you might already recognize the frustration of a lengthy process. Here's an example of the steps a large company might use to screen product or service acquisitions. Like a video game, you must be successful in each step to advance to a higher level.

1. Secretary screens caller on the phone.

2. If secretary hears value, literature is requested.
3. Literature is reviewed by manager.
4. Literature is shared with a team.
5. Sales rep is invited in to present.
6. Team peppers rep with questions.
7. Written proposal is requested.
8. Manager and team review proposal.
9. Team member assigned to beating up rep calls to do so.
10. Rep lowers price.

It never really ends, does it?

During this time frame, the rep has married, borne children, and sent them off to university.

Internal Processes

We don't all sell to large organizations, but it's good to know that a system like the one described above is in place in every buyer's brain. When responding to a *how* question, here's how a buyer might describe his or her internal process:

"I looked at your literature and was impressed, so I called you in to meet. Next, I ran my impressions of our conversation by some key people. They would normally recommend whether to try out your service. They weren't very enthusiastic. I then discussed it with my boss. She said, "Don't spend any money until we absolutely have to.""

The list would read like this:

1. I read your literature.
2. I discussed my impressions.
3. I then discussed it with my boss.

A pattern is emerging. This pattern reveals the path a buyer takes to come to a conclusion in his or her decision-making process. This buyer's initial step in analyzing information is visually oriented. The next step is to engage in verbal interaction. Noticing these two steps will give you some powerful insights into your prospect's personal decision-making model. The prospect has just revealed his or her individual blueprint for buying. This can help you sell the buyer more effectively. For further details on the working of the brain, see "Have a B.A.G.E.L. Five Bites to Selling Success," on page 161.

What do we do with this information? We want to match that buyer's patterns when we work with him or her. For example, the buyer would be very comfortable with a salesperson who said something like, "If I showed you how you could save forty percent of your prospecting time and, after conferring with your colleagues, it sounded like something worth discussing with your boss, would it make sense to have me at that meeting?"

When we travel a parallel decision-making path, we are walking alongside the buyer. This is extremely powerful because we are partnering with that person, not trying to convince him that our way is right or smart or best.

Caution: Most prospects will hear you asking *why*, even when you use the term *how*. They will give the quick answer and not describe the process you want to hear. You'll have to gently ask the question again, perhaps worded differently, but emphasizing *how*. You might need to tell the prospect that you are asking *how*, that is, asking what process he or she engages in to decide whether to take on a new product or service. *When you are doing this, point to your head!* The unspoken message to the buyer is that you're wondering how his mind works.

If you can determine the process a buyer uses to make purchasing decisions, you're light years ahead of your competition.

Take This Wisdom and Walk Away With It

Replace the word *why* with *how*. Do it today, and do it in your vocabulary at work and home. Isn't it a big personal bonus to understand how your family and friends make decisions? Pay close attention to the words you use and the words you feed to others. Your elevated communication skills will make you more money at work and draw you closer to people you care about.

Prospect Fades to Black as Sales Rep Rambles

JP shares how his dinosaur daddy loves to talk

MY FATHER WAS THE ONLY real estate agent in a small town in Canada. After school, I went to work with him for a few years. Those years were enough to teach me that selling was not meant for me.

My father had a client who would buy rundown houses, renovate them a little, and rent them for a small profit. This client came in one day to talk to my dad, who quickly ushered him into the closing room. As was his habit, Dad left the door open so that the rest of us agents could see and hear what a real closer was like.

Now, my father had a habit of rambling on and on and on. This day was no different, and as the afternoon wore on I could hear that Dad was trying to set the world rambling record. After two hours, I realized that I had not heard his client speak at all. The gentleman simply gazed out the window, nodding occasionally. I stepped into the office, hoping to save this unfortunate soul from any more of my father's prattling, when I noticed that his client was slumped in his chair and his color was ashen.

Unknown to any of us, Dad's client was diabetic and had lapsed into a semi-conscious state. Emergency care was immediately summoned, and the client ended up being released from the hospital after a few days.

My dad later admitted that he'd realized the client had become unresponsive. However, he chalked it up to the need to do more "selling."

POSTMORTEM

THINK OF THAT POOR PROSPECT's last image as his world faded to black — a salesman's mouth motoring along. God save us from longwinded salespeople. This is a perfect example of a flawed traditional sales approach, which is to dump information, lots of it, on the prospect. In fact, this "old school" agent believes that the more information you toss out there, the more likely some points will make an impression and cause the sale to close. I don't call that selling, I call it *hoping*. Here's an outstanding sales rule that should skip through your brain daily: Picture a face. The face contains one mouth and two ears. So the rule is that you listen twice as much as you speak. Ask intelligent questions, sit back, and let the prospect do the work.

The Fox and the Dinosaur
Replacing Primitive Principles

Jeffrey Fox reveals the origins of extinct sales tactics and offers your survival strategy out of the Ice Age.

SELLING THE OLD WAY IS DEFINITELY DEAD, if it ever lived. Selling the old way was to make lots of cold calls, use icebreakers to soften up the customer, regale the customer with features and benefits, knock the competitor, talk fast and talk the customer into buying.

Since 25% of all sales are made by self-informed customers it probably never mattered how ineffective old-style salespeople were... the 25% generated enough revenue to mask the mistakes.

Customers have always bought products to improve their economic position or to feel good or both. Salespeople must understand that *all they really sell is money.* They don't sell gaskets or gauges or controls: They sell the economic value the customer receives from the gasket or gauge. If the gauge allows the customer to fill an underground gasoline tank with enough gas to serve his or her buyers - *while not buying an extra 1000 gallons that sits unsold for three weeks* - then the gauge reduced the customer's investment in inven-

42

tory. *That inventory investment savings can be dollarized.* The effective salesperson dollarizes the value of the gauge and shows the customer that *the true cost of the gauge is the sales price minus the inventory savings.*

The modern salesperson sells a positive return on investment. The investment is what the customer pays for the product. The return is the economic benefit the customer receives from using the product.

Old selling is features and benefits. Real selling is dollarization.

Jeffrey Fox is the author of best-selling books, *How to Become a Rainmaker* and *How to Become CEO*. He can be found at Fox & Company, Inc. www.foxandcompany.com.

Owner Dies and Takes the Deal With Him

Ken describes digging the grave to bury his sale

I WAS WORKING FOR A COMPANY (the best in its industry) selling customized messages and music-on-hold. The prospect described himself as "ready to go." But he persisted on hiding behind voicemail, and I left messages that went unreturned for a few months. Finally, I got a human being, who informed me that the man I'd been trying to reach (the owner) had died the day after we had spoken.

I apologized, expressed my regrets, then (ready to pitch again) asked who was now in charge. It was the owner's son who was speaking to me. He didn't like the fact that I had so quickly moved from regrets to marketing. He told me never to call him again, even though he knew he could use our service.

SENSITIVITY TO THE INDIVIDUAL PROSPECT distinguishes good sales-people from bad ones. You don't speak the same to everyone you call on, do you? Remember Habit #5 of Stephen Covey's Seven Habits: Seek first to understand, then to be understood. A kind thing to do in this case would be to simply say, "This must be a tough time for your family. When might it be appropriate to call back?"

Expiration-Dated Advertising

The Wizard of Ads, Roy H. Williams, reveals the Dinosaur danger of using high-pressure tactics to sell

PEOPLE WHO REFER TO THE EARTH as "round" are technically wrong, but directionally accurate. Technically, our planet is an oblate spheroid. But to explain that subtle difference just wouldn't be worth the trouble, so we usually say, "the earth is round," and leave it at that.

The brain, you see, is a very smart organ.
It knows better than to transfer information
into long-term memory when that information is
flashing a "soon-to-expire" message in neon letters.

Likewise, what you're about to read is technically wrong, but directionally accurate.

For each of our senses, the brain offers short-term and long-term memory. Short-term memory is electrical. Long-term memory is chemical.

The objective of "branding" is to cause your product to be the one the customer thinks of first and feels best about when their moment of need arises. Consequently, branding must be accomplished in long-term memory. No problem — it's just a matter of repetition, right? Wrong. The brain, you see, is a very smart organ. It knows better than to transfer information into long-term memory when that information is flashing a "soon-to-expire" message in neon letters. I'm referring to ads that make a limited-time offer. When advertisers insist on trying to "whip people into action" with the urgency of a limited-time strategy, they can be sure that their message will never make it into long-term memory. At best, it will stay in short-term memory only until the expiration date has passed, and then it will be forever erased from the brain. Consequently, you cannot use a series of limited-time offers as the foundation for a long-term branding campaign.

The bottom line is, you can't have your cake and eat it, too. So, which kind of advertising will you do, short-term or long term? Will you have a little piece of cake right now, or a series of larger pieces later on? This is the choice that every advertiser makes, either consciously or unconsciously. I want you to make it consciously.

Yes, limited-time offers, when they work, cause people to take action immediately. The downside is that limited-time offers don't work better and better as time goes by. In truth, they work worse and worse. When an advertiser makes a limited-time offer, the only thing that goes into long-term memory is "This advertiser makes limited-time offers." In essence, the advertiser is training the customer to ask, "When does this go on sale?"

Will you invest your ad dollars in a long, slow, tedious branding campaign that will work better and better as time goes by, or will you do short-term, high impact, grab-for-the-brass-ring ads and look for a quick-hit payoff? Will you ride the tortoise … or the hare?

It's always your choice. Just know what you're choosing.

Roy H. Williams is the author of two amazing insightful books that you must own: *The Wizard of Ads* and *Secret Formulas of the Wizard of Ads*. Roy would like you to get your free subscription to "Roy's Monday Morning Memo" at http://www.WizardofAds.com.

Sales Tourist

Part Two

The Sales Tourist

THE SALES TOURIST IS UNPROFESSIONAL in words and action. In the selling profession, he or she might be distastefully described as 'amateur,' 'rookie,' or even 'bad seed.' The three reasons for this amateur behavior? This individual is probably:

New to selling
Poorly trained or untrained
Not taking the job/career very seriously

I use the term "tourist" because of a speech I heard. Of his visit to the Vietnam War Memorial in Washington, D.C., a great speaker said, "Watching people at that wall, you could tell the difference between the tourists and 'investors.' The tourists are gawking and talking at this magnificent work of art. They show little outward regard for the seriousness and significance of this monument. The investors are quiet and respectful. Many are on their knees. The names on the wall signify the ultimate investment, made by comrades and loved ones giving their lives."

Someone who's invested in something has a different set of behaviors than a sightseer just passing through. And so this behavior reflects the attitude the salesperson has chosen. I've never met a tourist-mentality salesperson who was any good at his or her craft.

Salesman Gets Caught Selling

*Tom tells of his
short trip into selling*

SHORTLY AFTER COLLEGE, I was selling over-the-counter drugs for a big multinational company.

My prospect one morning was a pharmacist/drugstore owner who'd listen to my pitch for fifteen seconds, then walk away to take care of a customer. Then he'd amble back and say, "Go ahead, keep talking."

I got sick of this after the fifth time, so when he walked away again, I stuffed my pockets full of razor blades, pens, gum, and some other handy items.

Eventually, he came back and told me to continue. I finally finished my pitch and he agreed to a very small order — about two hundred dollars' worth, which I thought was lousy.

"One more thing," he said. "Do you have any samples in your car?"

"Yes," I said. "Why?"

He told me that if I gave him all my samples, he wouldn't call the police and tell my employer. He'd somehow seen me shoplifting his stock. You'd better believe I emptied my trunk into his store! The moral of my story is simple: look carefully before you steal during a sales call.

POSTMORTEM

I WONDERED IF TOM was e-mailing me from prison. He's the ultimate example of a tourist in the trade of selling. Let Tom serve as a warning: Tourists don't stay in one place very long, do they? How long will you hang around in sales? If you get very serious about your life in selling, you'll earn more than you could in 90 percent of the jobs out there. You can learn from experts and shortcut your trip to success. You can study their behavior, read their books, and join organizations that attract these successful people. Are you really dedicated to a career in selling? Are you willing to go invest time, money, and energy in your journey to sales stardom? Decide today to travel this path, and your actions, attitudes, and earnings will reflect that investment.

Crying Over Spilled Ink

Scott speaks on being in the spotlight without knowing the cameras were rolling

ON A HOT DAY, I was in Florida with a partner. We were about to do a software demo to a large meeting at an office supply outfit. We were running a half hour late when we swung into the parking lot and pulled into the visitors spot, right in front of the stylish mirrored building.

As we got out, my very agitated partner notices that his pen had leaked on his shirt. He lost his temper, shouted swear words, whipped off his suit coat, and quite literally ripped his shirt off. Fabric tearing and buttons flying, he wadded it up and fired it in the nearby bushes. Bare-chested, sweating, and swearing, he tore though his luggage, got another shirt from the trunk, put it on, adjusted his tie in the mirrored office window, and we went in.

We called at first-floor reception and were led down the hall and into an already filled conference room.

I looked out the window and there was our car. My partner's shirt was still stuck in the bushes. Fifteen people important to our financial futures had had a ringside view of a terrific temper tantrum.

To this day, I'm very cautious in and around parking areas — no speeding, stealing parking spaces, illegal parking, etc. I'm "on" from the moment I drive into the customer's lot.

POSTMORTEM

LIKE CHILDREN, SALESPEOPLE sometimes need to be taught about consequences. Often, others are observing our actions when we least suspect it. Act like a pro, from the moment you get in the car to begin your day, until you get home at night. Remember that you're always sending a message to somebody, including yourself.

Customer on the Warpath

Dan discloses how his beer sales account relationship came to a head

A FEW YEARS BACK, while I worked for a mid-sized distributor of specialty beers, I experienced an incident that has made me especially careful of my language choices, and conscious of whom I am speaking to.

One day, my sales route took me to a casino, a very good, high-volume account. As it happens, a Native-American tribe operated this casino, and many of the employees and managers were, of course, members of that tribe. From having worked with them for a year, I was very comfortable with this account: I knew all the protocols, security checks, and rules, so I serviced them in a friendly, confident manner.

As I entered an area to access the cooler and take inventory, the woman whom I always saw greeted me. The first words out of my mouth were the ones that had become my standard greeting to *all* clients I felt comfortable with.

"How's it goin,' Chief?" I said, and stepped into the walk-in cooler.

Those four simple words meant the death of my services to that account. As I exited the cooler, an obviously perturbed woman intercepted me and said, "Some of the people who work here would probably be offended by what you just said, mister!"

My face immediately turned a brilliant shade of red! I'd never done anything so dumb before. Shaken, I stuttered an attempt at a most sincere apology, pleading for forgiveness. It was too late; I was asked, nicely, to leave.

At my office, I was informed that the customer had called and said, "If your company wishes to continue to do business with us, that racist salesman is not to enter the premises!"

I learned that when it comes to social procedure, business is business. Never allow yourself to become complacent just because you feel you "know" your client!

⚰ POSTMORTEM

How would you like to be Dan's sales manager, taking that phone call from an angry client? Here's how a good coach would handle Dan:

First, Dan already knows he blew the call, so there's no need to beat him up further. Ask him, obviously, to think carefully about his choice of words. But what about *any* words that sound insincere? Is "How's it going?" a sincere greeting? Most of the time, it's not. Say something meaningful, like "I love coming to your property." And, please, use the individual's name — the most precious sound to anyone.

Sales Pitcher Strikes Out on Mega-Deal

A sales trainer laments the loss of a bad student

MEGAN CAME TO ONE OF MY executive sales briefings, where I teach entrepreneurs and sales professionals how to significantly increase their effectiveness in selling. Megan claimed to understand the concept of "unpaid consulting," the process of dumping extremely valuable insights, even complex solutions, in front of a potential client before a relationship has been established. She agreed that unpaid consulting happens at times, but also believed that both showing off and being thorough were a big part of designing proposals.

But, Megan was involved in a *big deal,* and she just knew I was wrong about how to prepare and present proposals. She made a very detailed proposal on a sixty-four-million-dollar project. Her personal commission on the deal was three and a half million dollars! They loved her proposal. In fact they accepted it. But they bought the stuff from someone else. The company took apart her proposal and used it to craft their ideal solution. Then they began contacting companies in a lower price range than hers. Megan will always wonder who got her multimillion-dollar commission check.

 **POSTMORTEM**

WHEN YOU HAVE A GREAT MONTH, you might reward yourself with a gift or some extra personal time — a vacation trip to an island, perhaps. How would you treat yourself after a three-and-a-half-million-dollar bonus check? Megan never got to find out. She got suckered by a prospect who wanted to siphon her knowledge and shop her solution to someone cheaper. Be very careful before creating a "work of art" proposal of high quality and detail. Get very comfortable with your potential client before investing all that time and ink. You might just find yourself writing fewer proposals — and spending more pure selling time on higher-probability prospects.

The Ugliest Phrase in Selling

Thoughts on The Tourist

The number-one mistake that a Sales Tourist makes — actually, the bad news is that we've all done it, from the most experienced sales pro to the rookie with sixty days on the job — is doing *unpaid consulting,* the ugliest phrase in selling.

Unpaid consulting happens in two ways in the selling world: in person and in print.

In Person: Face To Face and Phone Calls

The easiest path to a prospect presentation is to do an information dump. This usually takes the form of an offering of features and benefits. This spewing of information then sets the stage for a prospective client to suck out all the juicy details of your offering.

Think about it. You're shopping. What do you do when you have lots of information, perhaps even a good solution to your problem? Do you ever buy immediately from the person pitching you? No, you drain every last drop of detail about the sales rep's solution to your problem. Then you do one of two things: shop some more or fix it yourself. You do this because, personally, you could save time and money. On the job, you'd better make the best choice when it comes to solutions for your company's trouble, or others might question your decision-making ability.

For example, when I was younger, I'd try to fix a car problem myself rather than pay an auto repair shop to do it. *But I needed a diagnosis first.* If I could get a diagnosis, I could repair the car myself. I'd visit the library for the car book (why buy it?), go to an auto parts store (why pay retail price to the garage?), and then fix it (why pay someone fifty dollars an hour?).

Here's a painful fact that you already know: Unless you have a unique product or are first on the block, there are plenty of ways that cost less to solve the problem than the solution you're selling. Salespeople are often blind-sided by this buyer data-gathering process. Buyers get a good solution from you (thanks!), then keep shopping.

Each day, thousands of reps perform this "backwards" manner of handling sales calls.

Unpaid consulting will kill your career. Decide what information you can share and what information you get paid for. It's that simple. Don't believe that being a nice person and a great conversationalist will generate a sale. You do most of the talking, and fail to find out what the buyer's real problem is. Then you walk away feeling great, only to realize later that your hopes of closing that prospect were false. Each day, thousands of reps perform this "backwards" manner of handling sales calls.

The emotional stress such false hope places on you is tremendous. Your gut will actually get you out of the selling business before your lack of earnings does, because you'll find yourself chasing prospects who'll either hide behind voicemail or continue to stall you.

In Print: Marketing Literature Mayhem

Here's a story you might find interesting and useful. The vice president of sales for one of the four major credit card companies was a good friend. She was showing the new corporate literature for some upcoming ad campaigns, and I just shook my head. "Your marketing people don't get it. They all have MBAs and know the hottest color to use, which fonts are catchy, and how slick to make the paper. But they don't understand how to write."

"What's wrong with this?" she asked. "We need to educate the financial industry and the public about our new products."

I told her that the kiss of death for businesses — big and small — is to believe that their efforts are about education. Marketing efforts should be about *motivation*. Motivation to take action.

"Get some college kids, dump the MBAs, and make the new hires read Dr. Jeffrey Lant's book *Cash Copy*. They won't need any more education than that. I'm dead serious."

She'd never heard of the book, so I loaned her mine at the next opportunity.

Of course, she couldn't replace the MBAs (not her call), and she couldn't replace the incorrect marketing messages that had been burned into their brains by school. It's the classic battle of education vs. reality: Does what works in the classroom work in the workplace? If it did, graduates would always walk into hundred-thousand-dollar marketing jobs, because their expertise would make millions for their companies. Learn to study what really works. (You never actually do get *out* of school anyway, do you?) Collect mailing pieces that get your attention, and incorporate their design and language concepts. Remember that marketing is really another name for lead generation.

If you're an entrepreneur or manager who creates literature to increase sales, remember that education should not come before motivation. Tantalize those readers briefly, then motivate them to take some action: call, visit your website, or mail back your reply card. That will make you more money than educating will. For another view of the education vs. motivation question, just think about the difference in earnings between teachers and sales professionals. That's a sad and brutal reality, because many teachers often work harder and invest in much more education toward their trade than salespeople do.

Don't be a sales pro or entrepreneur who loses by educating prospects. Make motivation to action your number-one priority in person and in print. Avoid *unpaid consulting* and you'll avoid the headaches and ulcers that accompany it.

Killer Joke Kills a Sale

Brian explains how his humorous comment called for his casket

I WAS WORKING FOR A MANUFACTURER covering Florida. On my first visit to a potential dealer, I sat in his office reviewing our product line. The prospect received a phone call from the police department regarding a recent incident. Trying to add a little humor to the situation, I commented, "Gee, I hope you're not a murderer."

He didn't answer, so I quickly decided to change the subject and focus on the picture of his wife and daughter on the credenza behind his desk. "I see you have a beautiful daughter. How old is she?" The prospect looked at me with a somber face and replied, "She was ten. She and her mother were killed two months ago in a vehicle accident." Well, now I knew what the "incident" was.

Could it be worse? Oh yes. I learned on the way out the door that he had also been driving the vehicle. Needless to say, my relationship with this customer never even got started — it crashed and burned without a sound.

Talk about opening mouth and inserting foot. Never had anything like that happened in my ten years of selling. Besides feeling like a real jerk, I was thinking of my own daughter and how I would have felt. Walking through the parking lot I mumbled a few four-letter words to myself for stepping outside the boundaries of professionalism.

Never again would I discuss anything outside of business unless the customer brought it up first. I now keep my little jokes to myself, and let the customer decide if he or she wishes to talk on a casual level.

BRIAN FELL INTO THE TRAP of treating a new relationship like a comfortable, friendly one. His questions assume that a good rapport is already being built. He's wrong. Please be careful about crossing personal boundaries with a stranger. Yes, it's frustrating to have a sales call interrupted by a call or visit. It's also very rude to the salesperson, but you've had that happen from time to time, haven't you? A wiser comment when this occurs is to ask whether this is a bad time to talk. If the response is yes, be prepared to leave, but not without booking your new appointment.

Olympic Vision Freezes Out Salesman

Jeff laments his loss of new business and the existing work, too

IT BEGAN AS AN INNOCENT LUNCH with my partner and possibly the biggest client we would ever get. It was back in the eighties during the winter Olympics, when the U.S. women's luge team was finally competitive. They also sported blue nylon speed suits for the first time. If you recall the suits, they were skintight, and you could always tell what was or wasn't worn underneath.

I hadn't met the client's boss, but he was coming to lunch, too. My client was a bit on the ribald side, and we had shared jokes and stories about the opposite sex, so I knew he was no prude.

I was the last of the four to arrive at the expensive restaurant. They rose to shake hands, but instead of introducing the boss by name, my partner started by saying, "Did you see the Olympics on TV last night?" Well, I had. Then he said, "Did you see Karen B. (not her real name)?"

Well, I had. She was a vision in skintight blue nylon, so I proceeded to say something like, "Wow, did I ever! She was so gorgeous that if she were a blueberry Popsicle (which she reminded me of), I would have licked that blue right off her."

There was a short silence, and my partner finished the introductions with, "Well, I'd like you to meet her father, Mr. John B."

The dad, who was at least a foot taller than I, did not seem too upset, but of course I was squirming through the entire lunch. The aftermath however, was chiseled in stone. In the end, not only did we not get the contract, but we also lost all the other business we'd been doing with "dad's" firm. I will never again interrupt an introduction.

 POSTMORTEM

OKAY, THIS IS AN EASY ONE. Avoid lewd, rude comments at all times. Jeff is a verbal tourist who speaks without thinking because he's not going to be around this location long. How do you know where to draw the line in making what you think are "funny" comments? Just assume that you're calling on Mother Teresa. And remember that it takes more intelligence to use clean humor than to end up in the gutter like a misdirected bowling ball. It's almost always a good move for a salesperson to use proper humor. If the buyer enjoys your company, it's easier to sell that individual. However, you might as a rule ask yourself, "Would I say this to my mother?" to decide if your amusing comments are appropriate.

Boating Blunder Sinks Deal

Vince vocalizes how his sales manager is unconvincing

THIS WAS MY MOST PAINFUL sales experience: I was engineering manager for a consulting firm. We had been discussing a long-term retainer program with a major boating equipment manufacturer. It appeared that all the pieces were in place as their director of engineering invited us to spend the afternoon wrapping things up as we cruised Lake Michigan on one of their corporate boats.

Accompanying me was our corporate sales manager, who never hid his opinion that engineers can't sell, and professional salespeople need to close deals. The afternoon started off great. Our host told me that if his group leader signed off on our proposal, it was a go. Mixed in with a discussion of business, the director of engineering, a proper southern gentleman type, pointed out some beaches that were cleaned up under his organization in his role as volunteer park superintendent.

As we approached Navy Pier in Chicago, it was looking like our sales manager had had too much to drink. That was made clear when he dropped his shorts and exposed his backside to a passing harbor cruise ship. Quietly, I tried to tell him to sit down and shut up, but on the small boat, this type of communication was difficult. Unfortunately, he "mooned" another cruise ship.

Business talk had dried up by that point, though I wasn't sure if it was because of the sales manager's antics or that we were just finished. I kept my fingers crossed, and nothing else happened until we finally docked.

As we moored the boat, the sales manager finished another bottle of beer, and tossed the empty into the harbor! Remembering our host's efforts on park reclamation, and knowing that there was no way I was going to be able to retrieve that bottle, I just hoped it wasn't noticed. Back in the parking lot, I was trying to clarify the next step, hoping our sales guy would just keep quiet as he swayed back and forth with his eyes half shut.

59

I got my wish, but watched in horror as he finished yet another beer and tossed the can into the adjacent park — with trash cans two steps away. I retrieved the can and disposed of it properly, but was pretty sure we'd blown it.

That was confirmed when, after trying to reach the director of engineering for three days, I was informed that their company really wasn't interested in a retainer program — but thanks for our time.

What lessons did I learn? Well, I got out of that company and started my own with some other people I respect. Our sales manager's company recently filed bankruptcy and is now a memory.

 POSTMORTEM

TOO BAD VINCE couldn't have "accidentally" pushed his sales manager overboard — it might've saved the sale. Respect is really the issue in this tale. The drunken manager had no respect for his colleague, the prospect, or his own company. Who would want to work with or do business with someone who trashes the basic principles of courtesy? For a healthier sales career, learn to honor those you call on and work with. You'll find your personal life rewarded, too.

Sales Rep Hurting
for Cash Aims High

*Sales manager Ray
describes a "blown" bank deal*

WE HAD A COMPANY in Massachusetts that sold advertising to banks. One of our sales reps was six feet two inches tall, redheaded, and could be described as "highly visible." Banks in Massachusetts were open on Saturdays, and one Saturday morning our tall redhead walked into one of his client banks, carrying what appeared to be a long cardboard box for a flower arrangement.

He sat at the advertising officer's desk, one end of the box resting on the floor and the other pointed toward the ceiling.

The ad officer smiled and said something like, "To what do we owe the pleasure of this Saturday visit?"

"I'm here to rob the bank," announced our redheaded salesman.

Laughter follows — until redhead reaches through a hole cut in the side of the flower box and — boom! — he fires a shotgun round into the bank's ceiling.

Pandemonium results, during which our trusty rep scoops up some cash, scrambles out the door and into his station wagon, and makes a clean getaway — until the state police block him five miles down the turnpike and arrest him.

Afterward, of course, the president of our company is in complete panic. The news of this event will ruin our business with banks, he believes.

I rush to the rescue. As sales manager, I can smooth things over by quickly introducing the replacement salesman to the very same bank. The new guy is champing at the bit to prove himself. The bank knows our company (obviously), so we're ushered in immediately. Our eager new man wants to be respectful of the banker's time, and blurts out a very unfortunate choice of words: "Well, we wouldn't want to hold you up!" The banker steps back, his face registering fear and his eyeballs get bigger, as I leap in saying, "No, no. What we meant ..."

Forget it. Disaster, no recovery possible, only an awkward with-drawal and mumbled words about "checking back with you soon."

☠ POSTMORTEM

WOW! HERE'S A REAL SALES TOURIST. Rob a client to solve one's financial problems? Did you know that there are great assessment tools you can use to measure a salesperson's potential success? You can also measure how likely any sales rep is to learn new selling strategies. If you're a manager, this might keep you from hiring a potential bank robber. If you're a salesperson wondering how much money you can really make in your field, it might help you decide "How high is high?". One of the best assessments I've experienced in twenty-plus years of sales and sales management is Dave Kurlan's testing tool. A free assessment is available to readers of this book at www.objectivemanagement.com/SalesAssessment.htm.

Dave also has a fascinating article on anticipating your selling success based on how well you make buying decisions (See his article "Can You Pedal Your Sales Cycle at a Higher Speed?", page 66). Find a way to keep out of Tourist mode. Be serious about being a professional and you will certainly avoid explosions that can damage your business.

Old Salesmen Never Die

Eric remarks, "Never rip your competition, they might be neighbors."

COMPETITION TO SELL multimillion-dollar buildings in Los Angeles is ferocious. The name of the game in this business is getting listings. Once you've got listings, other agents help you earn your commission. There are also many very old, very experienced agents to compete with in this mature market. When I heard another young agent use a closing technique to get a listing, I began to copy it on my sales calls.

So there I was in my best suit, best tie, and polished shoes, sitting in front of one of those big-dollar building owners. As my final, major benefit, I explained my technique. "Look, I'm not like those *old guys* in this business. They just slap two signs on your building and wait for the phone to ring. I'm aggressive; I'll find buyers, good buyers for you." The owner thanked me for my time and said he'd take that specific comment under consideration.

Several hours later, I returned to my office to find a note on my desk to see my sales manager — another guy who'd been in the business for decades. He waved a document in front of me.

"Eric," he said, "about your sales call this morning — a couple of *old guys* from *this* office just got the listing."

The building owner had repeated my closing technique to some of my fellow salesmen. The manager then proceeded to humiliate me (thank God we were alone), telling me to never knock the competition and to show respect for the guys who paved the way for me by building this company's reputation. Now I had the uncomfortable future of working with the 'old guys' who had captured the listing.

And I stopped using that closing technique. I had learned two things: never rip the competition, and sometimes closing techniques can backfire.

ERIC DID TWO THINGS WRONG: First, as he noted, he made a negative comment about his competition. Next, he told his prospect what he was going to do. When you want to make a statement, turn it into a question. Here's how: "Mr. Prospect, most agents simply slap two signs on your building and wait for the phone to ring. I'm aggressive; I'll find buyers, good buyers for you. Is that the kind of person you'd like to work with?"

The buyer then affirms or denies your approach: "Yes, time is an issue" (now you'd better find out exactly what that means) or, "No, I don't like aggressive, pushy types representing me" (better discuss that, too). You've tested the waters with a question instead of putting yourself in a box. Change as many statements as you can into questions, and get the prospect talking more today.

The Opposite of Blessed Is Banished

Jeff, in engineering sales, tells his tale of revenge on a sales guy

THE SUPPLIER HAD DECIDED to schmooze a fellow engineer and me with a free lunch. The three of us climbed into this vendor's car and, as we left his plant, he asked where we'd like to eat. "Anywhere is great," he added. "Except no *gook* food."

As a father of an adopted Korean daughter, I decided to advise him that he might be a little too vocal about his prejudices.

Yes, I was angry enough to eat his "free lunch" both literally and figuratively. The thickheaded bigot was about to really pay. He was one of our suppliers, and we sold his parts to our clients. He was so dense that he never caught on that I de-sourced him that afternoon: wouldn't you know it — his parts ended up disappearing from our catalog!

He would come see me and complain about how orders from us were down. He'd bitch about the economy and all sorts of other reasons, never realizing that his mouth had been the cause. Not only was he oblivious to my feelings as his customer, but he never even asked me why sales were down. He just made his own conclusions and got stuck in that reality.

I don't know if he ever learned how poorly he'd managed our sale. Some people don't belong in a sales role anyway.

POSTMORTEM

WOULD YOU BUY SOMETHING from a tourist? Would you invest your money in a person who was a temporary relationship? The supplier placed himself into this category when he revealed his true feelings about "foreigners." He paid dearly for it. Remember the old principle that says, "People buy from people they like." It's entirely true. Jeff could never enjoy working with someone so ignorant of his personal situation. Learn two things here:

Get to know your prospect's likes and dislikes over time, and *Create conversations that build people up.*

People want to hang out with someone who cares about these two items, and many people even want to buy from them.

Can You Pedal Your Sales Cycle at a Higher Speed?

Sales force assessment specialist Dave Kurlan's business is built around the ability to pinpoint the trouble with Sales Tourists and knowing whether they can be salvaged for selling success.

Selling is a self-fulfilling prophecy. Time and again, you'll get your prospects to behave in a manner that's consistent with how you would behave in a similar situation. These expectations make up your brain's "digital programming," those permanently recorded messages that program your performance.

Pedaling a bicycle may be the most important element in your digital programming. First, we change the spelling from *bicycle* to *Buy Cycle*. Use the same pronunciation as before, but place a tremendous degree of importance on your Buy Cycle. Your Buy Cycle, or how *you* would normally go about the business of making a major purchase, will predetermine the kind of sell cycle you'll have when you *sell* to your prospects.

Steve said that his last major purchase was a diamond engagement ring for his fiancée'. It cost $1100, took him thirteen months to buy it, and took him to twenty-seven different stores.

Steve, a young mortgage originator, came to me for help awhile back. Steve said that his last major purchase had been a diamond engagement ring for his fianc e. It cost eleven hundred dollars, it took him thirteen months to buy, and took him to twenty-seven different stores. He was searching for the lowest price, didn't believe in financing, and made six trips back to the store where he finally bought. For Steve, a major purchase was anything more than fifty dollars and Steve sold mortgages for a bank!

When he came to me, Steve had just finished a terrible year in which he earned only thirty-five hundred dollars. He didn't understand why he was failing, and he hoped I could make a difference. I couldn't, and here's why:

If we were to put Steve in front of his typical prospects, the setting would be a young couple's living room, where they are about to finance their first home. You can already see one of the problems here, as Steve doesn't believe in financing. He pays cash for everything!

Steve moves through the sales call as he always does, and comes to the close (one I'm sure was pretty weak). His prospects say, "Steve, you're the first person we've spoken to ... we really need to see what else is out there."

Steve could have fifty great techniques for handling the "We want to shop around" objection, but he won't use them because he understands their thinking; he buys into it. That's what he would do too. That's great bonding at the cost of closing!

Maybe they say, "Steve, you quoted us a rate of eight and a half percent, but we saw an ad in today's paper for eight and a quarter percent at ABC Mortgage Company. We always go with the best price."

Steve would, too, even if it took thirteen months to find it! This is yet another example of a situation where the salesperson could have umpteen techniques for handling a price objection, but won't use any of them effectively, or at all, because he understands. Dead Again!

Perhaps the prospects tell Steve, "We never make a decision the first time we see anything!"

Does Steve spring into action here? No. Steve wouldn't make a decision the first time, either. Or the second, third, or fourth time. Steve can't make decisions, so how in the world will he help others make them? He won't. Yet more powerful techniques go unused!

Here's a good one: The couple says, "You know, we always pay cash for everything, we don't really like payments, we only got credit cards to build our credit so that we'd be able to get a mortgage, but we don't even use them. We're really uncomfortable signing our lives away for thirty years!"

As you recall, Steve doesn't believe in financing either, so what's he even doing in this business? Who hired this guy?

Here's one more he can't handle: "Gee Steve, this is really a lot of money!" It's only $249,950 more than a lot of money to Steve (on a $250,000 mortgage). Remember Steve believes a major purchase is more than fifty dollars.

Steve was failing miserably in this business because he shouldn't have been there in the first place! His Buy Cycle is totally non-supportive of his sell cycle, resulting in repeated failures. With an awful and self-limiting Buy Cycle like Steve's, he shouldn't even be in sales. I believe that the most significant piece of past programming in a salesperson's brain is his or her Buy Cycle.

The Ten Crucial Elements in Your Buy Cycle

1. *Money Tolerance* At what dollar amount does something become a major purchase for you?

The lower this number, the more vulnerable you will be to the objection "That's a lot of money." You understand, so you'll tend to let the prospect off the hook. In contrast, the higher this number becomes for you personally, the more effectively you'll deal with prospects who say this, because you'll be less likely to understand their perception.

2. *Time Line* How much time passed between when you first thought about making a purchase and when you actually bought?

How long it takes you to actually buy what you want is directly proportional to how long it could take you to get your prospect to do business with you. Your prospect procrastinates, puts off making a decision, puts it on the back burner, or says it isn't a priority. You understand. The less time you invest in making a purchase, the harder it is for you to understand this stall. You'll make a better argument and your sell cycle will be shorter.

3. *Potential for Getting Your Brain Picked for Free* Do you have a need to do research before you buy?

If you research, visit salespeople to become educated, or you read *Consumer Reports* prior to buying, then you are extremely vulnerable to the prospect who wants to be educated. This person will usually pick your brain, determine what he needs, and then buy it from someone else for less money. You're liable to give too many inappropriate presentations. You understand. If you don't have this need to perform research, you'll have less tolerance for the prospects who want to do it to you, and won't let them do it without some commitment that you'll do business together.

4. *Competitive Vulnerability* How many stores will you shop, or how many salespeople will you invite in?

The more you need to comparison shop, the more you'll find yourself in that situation with your prospects. You understand. If you can just go to one store and buy it, you'll have an easier time keeping the competition out of your way.

5. *Profit Vulnerability* How do you decide from which store to purchase?

If you buy from the store where you can get the lowest price, you're in deep trouble: you'll be very vulnerable to the prospect who only buys the lowest price. You will either cut profits to make the sale, or determine that you can't make the sale unless your price is lowered. You understand. If, on the other hand, you choose from the store that's most helpful, or that sells the best product, or offers the best solution, or provides the best service, then you'll be much more effective with the prospect who wants to shop for price.

6. *Closing Power* How many trips will you make to that store before plopping down your cash, check, or credit card?

If you think things over prior to buying, then you'll be very vulnerable to the prospect who wants to think about it. You understand. If you can look at a product and buy it right then and there, then with proper style and bravery, you have the potential to be in closing encounters of the superstar kind.

7. *Customer Loyalty* Do you continue buying from the same store on a regular basis?

If you buy from different vendors or stores all the time, you'll find yourself with customers who do the same to you. You understand. If you're the loyal customer of a store or company you buy from, chances are you'll have a loyal following yourself.

8. *Referral Potential* Do you give quality referrals to salespeople?

If you neglect to take care of and refer others to the salespeople from whom you buy, you'll be desperate for quality referrals. You understand. If you do refer others, you'll develop a strong referral base, eliminating the need for endless cold calls.

9. *Sob Story Vulnerability* Is money tight for you?

Your prospects tell you they want what you have, but they just don't have the money. They say that money has really been tight. If that sounds familiar to you, you're vulnerable to that stall. You understand. If you can spend the money, you're more likely to help the prospect spend money on you.

10. *Killer Instinct* Will you find a way to pay for something you want even if you don't have the money?

If you always wait till the money is there, you'll allow your prospect to do the same. You understand. If you'll find a way to find the money, then chances are good that you expect your prospects to do the same thing.

Would you like to assess the impact your Buy Cycle is having on your selling career? Readers of this book can obtain a free assessment for salespeople and managers at

www.objectivemanagement.com/SalesAssessment.htm.

Dave Kurlan is the founder and president of the premier salesperson and sales manager assessment tool. He is also the author of *Mindless Selling*, available at www.1stbooks.com.

Sales Napoleon

Part Three

Sales Napoleon

THE SALES NAPOLEON lets ego get in the way of his or her business relationships. This is evident in three ways:

A selfish desire to win at all costs
A bad attitude that might include angry flare-ups
An inflated ego that won't ask for help

Napoleon, of course, has stood the test of time as a leader with a magnificent ego. When salespeople bring an arrogant attitude to the job, they reveal how they feel about themselves, their prospects, their company, their co-workers, and their product. This self-centered approach to the world creates win-lose relationships that can destroy sales performance.

Doctor Surgically Removes Commission:

National sales manager Bill shares how he was blindsided by Doctor Evil

TALK ABOUT A LONG SALES CALL: A rep and I had just spent seven hours in a prestigious New York doctor's office, applying our equipment to almost every patient who had an appointment. The medical diagnostic equipment we sold was best demonstrated on patients, and this particular day, we worked like dogs!

Finally, as it was getting dark outside, the doctor came up to me and said, "I'm ready to buy, but I only want to deal with you, not the sales rep."

"Why?" I ask. Of course, he's setting himself to negotiate with the "boss," and to tell me that he "wants the best price and won't pay anything that includes any commissions!"

He said just that, and concluded that he'd sign today, but not if he had to spend a dollar over a price that included commissions. He told me this right in front of the sales rep, after we had spent *seven hours* working his office. What nerve! He acted like the rep didn't even exist.

I replied, "But, doctor, this man works on straight commission, and we just spent the whole day here! I can't do that."

The doctor replied, "Look, you want a sale? Those are the ground rules … take it or leave it!"

The rep looked sheepishly at me. I secretly winked at him, turned to the doctor, and said, "Okay, I guess we'll cut the deal your way."

Earlier, we had discussed some pricing that included a hefty commission for my rep. The doctor didn't really know what price was rock bottom, so behind closed doors (with the rep abandoned in the hall), the doctor and I negotiated the deal. He signed the contract, confident he had gotten a steal and not the least bit concerned that the rep had been cut out of his share. The doctor then opened the door and walked right past my invisible rep and down the hall to see his next patient.

As the doctor disappeared into the examination room, I told the rep what deal was struck, and the rep immediately recognized a generous commission for himself. We giggled and started to high-five each other, celebrating in the hallway, laughing and dancing.

What we didn't notice was that the doctor had come out to get a chart, and was able to see us doing our celebration dance at the other end of the hall. Imagine what he was thinking: "Why is that rep happy with no commission? What's the deal?"

We hurried out only to get blind-sided a week later, when the lease payments were canceled and the sale was stopped. Seven hours of work for both of us went down the drain.

WHEN WAS THE LAST TIME you won an argument with a friend or a client by shouting, "I'm much smarter than you!"? Isn't this exactly what Bill, wearing his Napoleon hat, had done? He didn't tell the doc to his face, but "declared" it loudly enough for the soon-to-be-ex-client to hear. Keep your ego and excitement under wraps till you've closed the prospect. And don't forget: a prospect is not a client when he or she signs on the dotted line. A prospect becomes a client *when his check clears the bank.* Save your emotional outbursts until that money moves from their account into yours. You'll avoid buyer — and seller's — remorse.

The Difficulty of Selling to a Sleeping Prospect

John laments that he loses when his prospect snoozes

As A NEWLY HIRED manufacturer's rep, I was taking over a sales territory from my boss. I made a call with enthusiasm and confidence to sell our electrical products to a business owner. I knew that closing a deal my boss had started would be a "slam dunk." All I had to do was show up, deliver a brochure on the product, make a ten-minute presentation, and presto! I would receive the purchase order.

When I was invited to the customer's extravagant office, he told me to sit in a chair in front of his desk to deliver my information. I did, but about thirty seconds into it, he started to fall asleep! Head bobbing, one eye open, head falling backward, yawning, the whole nine yards. After about two minutes of distracted, one-way communication, I asked him if he would like me to come back another time. He alertly said no and told me to continue. Then he proceeded to fall deeply asleep. Confused and embarrassed, I dropped my information on his desk and left.

Later that afternoon, he called my boss and asked why I had left. He felt I was rude, given his condition, and that his dog — who barks at him when he falls asleep — was at the vet's.

I asked my boss, "What condition?"

"Oh, didn't I tell you? He has narcolepsy (a disease that makes you fall asleep)."

And I thought it was my presentation skills. Now, I always ask more questions before I start to sell.

 ## POSTMORTEM

LIKE ALL GREAT STORIES, this paints a colorful picture. John had a miserable selling experience because he was embarrassed; his ego was hurt. Rather than slinking away, John should have left the prospect's office and spoken to another person in the company about how to handle this unusual situation. He would have avoided embarrassing the prospect and having his boss receive an angry call. Here's the lesson: Don't let your ego prevent you from requesting help — at any point in the sales cycle. You might be surprised at how sympathetic and generous others can be.

Scent of a Salesperson

David whines that he wins a battle and loses the war

ONE DAY, LIKE MANY DAYS OF COLD CALLING, I entered a small upscale women's boutique. I was selling, with confidence, advertising space for a local directory. I was generally gifted in immediately identifying owners of smaller businesses.

When I entered the store, a heavy cloud suddenly darkened a showroom that was empty of customers. Three attractive attendants pretended not to notice me lurking at the entryway. I was patient. I'd been standing and walking all day; this was my air-conditioned opportunity to pick the owner out of the shy crowd.

At last, I spotted her glaring at me from the far reaches of the intimate room. As I waited for her to approach, I could see her mind plotting a line she would use to kick the obvious peddler out of her store. As she arrogantly parked herself inches from me, her opening comment was, "Can you smell that strong odor?"

My posture internally broke for a few moments as I attempted to calculate a comeback. I finally responded by lifting my nose to the air and proclaiming, "Yes, it smells delightful in here."

Immediately, she responded, "No, it smells like a salesman in here!"

It was time to change the direction of attack in this game. My best defense was asking her a question. I pointed to the clothes hanging on the racks and said, "Let me ask you a question: Is this a dry cleaner?"

"*No!* This is an upscale ladies' boutique!"

"Am I correct in assuming that you are the owner of such a fine establishment, but these articles of clothing are not for sale?"

"Why of course I'm the owner, and I sell more of my inventory than all my helpers combined."

My counter-attack was staged. "So you must be the source of the foul smell you mentioned earlier."

She finally laughed and allowed me to go into my pitch.

Even though I had broken through her barrier of communication,

I would never sell this lady a thing. As I exited the store on my journey to my next battle, I had to lift my arm to determine whether my deodorant truly had eight-hour protection as advertised.

 POSTMORTEM

ON ANY SALES ENCOUNTER, one of the toughest temptations to avoid is the desire to be right. David won the battle but lost the war. That is, he didn't close the sale. Traditional selling techniques that teach us to have a ready response to objections are at fault and can hurt our earnings badly. These responses can create an argumentative environment. When a prospect makes an objection and you can fire off a response so quickly and smoothly, you make the potential buyer feel dumb by saying, in effect, "You ask an obvious question that all the common folk ask, so, Mr. or Ms. Prospect, here's the obvious answer." That's a big mistake. Try this idea, instead: when someone attacks you, fall back with a reply like, "Wow, you probably have some good reasons for feeling that way; do you want me to leave?" Often the attacker will reverse position (hopefully feeling terribly guilty for treating a complete stranger so rudely) and invite you in.

You Get None from the Nuns

Frank confesses that he can't convert the convent

I WORKED IN THE TELECOMMUNICATIONS industry, selling phone systems to small businesses. One of the managers I worked with was a "knuckle buster," a hard closer type. His strategy was to lean up on the table on his knuckles and then growl at the prospect to close the deal — an approach exactly the opposite of mine.

We were selling a phone system to a convent, and I had done most of the preliminary work on setting up the sale. My manager demanded to attend this final meeting. He felt I had taken too much time with my "consultant" style of selling.

We walked into a conference room full of nuns. I explained the various features and benefits of the system, and then asked if there was anything standing in the way of us doing business. One of the nuns said that they'd need final approval from the bishop before they could sign the deal. At this, my manager rose up on his knuckles and roared, "Well then, what the hell am I doing here?"

Predictably, we were immediately escorted off the premises, politely, but without a sale.

I learned that in a sales call, any influence that goes against my own personal style only offers disastrous consequences.

 **POSTMORTEM**

TEAM SELLING CAN BE TROUBLE. Egos can endanger the sales call because each individual feels that he or she has value and insight to offer the buyer. The problem is that both team members have different experiences, personalities, and thought processes. Confusion often occurs when both people speak during the call. Even if they have identical sales training (sadly, a rare experience), they would tend to lead the buyer down different paths, each path a reflection of the direction each speaker feels the call should be going. For example, while doing software sales, I was asked to bring another rep with me on a sales call. During the conversation, he asked the buyer a question that completely derailed my selling process. It was a good question, and it deserved an answer, but it was the wrong time to ask. I never recovered the rapport I'd been building with the prospect. Upon returning to our office, the rep insisted that what he'd done was okay, and added that the idea that I had to be in "rapport" with a prospect was garbage. Though I was selling four times the product he was, his ego dug in its heels and insisted its owner was right.

How would I coach this fairly common scenario? Only one person works the prospect. The other guy says hello and sits silently. You should decide who must shut up, and that person is never allowed to say anything (unless the wastebasket catches fire — and even then his response must take the form of a question).

Printer Doesn't Get Bid, Calls Client a Cheat

Marcia reports that she is accused of manipulating salespeople

TWO COMPANIES WERE BIDDING for the job of printing a very complicated form. The proposal was for several thousand copies of a very complex two-page form, with multiple carbon-less copies of each page. It involved quite a bit of design, and had to be done carefully so that everything lined up correctly.

I asked the two major printers of business forms in our region to work up bids. I waited until both bids were in before opening either. The salesperson who didn't get the job was furious. He accused me of simply using him to get a bid that I then revealed to the competition to drive down their price. I hadn't done that, and I was hurt and angry at being accused of doing something so underhanded.

To this day I remember the deep emotion attached to this long-ago incident, and wonder if he deliberately threw a fit to get me to give him the job out of pity or remorse. As it turned out, both bids were so close that if he had expressed disappointment in a gentler manner, I probably would have made sure to give him the job the next time, thus giving both printers some of our business. But I was so turned off by his angry attitude that I simply resolved never to do business with his company again.

 POSTMORTEM

IT'S AMAZING HOW SOME memories are just burned into our brains (and our stomachs) because of the emotion generated by a bad situation. I asked Marcia if she had ever shared the experience with the rep's boss. She hadn't and admitted she should have. Here's my lesson on dealing with a bad sales rep relationship. I learned it at my wedding, so you can expect it was both memorable and painful. We had a bad wedding videographer (his description of his experience was better than the videotape revealed it to be), and were disgusted enough to tell all our friends and family. The best thing anyone suggested was that we complain to the church that had recommended this video person. I asked why I should squawk about it. "Imagine how many other wedding memories they'll ruin if you don't reveal the truth." Don't tolerate bad attitudes or service from salespeople, and please tell someone in their firm why you won't do business with them. You'll be doing that company a favor by pointing out some bad teeth that need extracting.

How to Keep Your CEO from Passing Out on Sales Calls

A security firm loses track of its leader

OUR PRESIDENT, CRAIG, is diabetic. Occasionally, we've struggled with his condition when it affected our sales calls. We had landed an appointment at a paper company; a ninety-six-thousand-dollar investigation contract was on the line. Craig was starting to fade on us. When his blood sugar begins bottoming out, we insist that he eat something. We insist this so that he doesn't take out a hypodermic syringe and shoot up in front of potential clients.

Anyway, the company's general manager was talking when Craig began sneaking bites of a sandwich he'd hidden beneath the board-room table. We hoped the guy wouldn't notice, but he stopped talking, grinned, and asked, "Craig, do you have enough for all of us?"

It was embarrassing. In the past, Craig had once begun acting drunk when he needed his medicine. He was doing the talking and began rambling, switching the subject from business to baseball. Another time, his condition hit him while he was tailing a suspect during a mobile surveillance job. We had to "run him down" in his own car to keep him from killing anyone. It hasn't occurred, but I'd bet that killing a client or suspect is very bad for business.

The guy at the paper company was gracious when we explained what was happening. But we didn't get his business. I didn't really blame him. I'd be a little nervous signing a contract with a vendor who has a problem like that — you know, wondering if he'd always be able to perform for a company laying out a hundred grand.

It was the final straw for this lesson: from now on, Craig would take care of his condition before meetings, or excuse himself — without explanation — during them.

 **POSTMORTEM**

EGOS ARE LIKE BIG TERMITES that eat away at the structure of a business relationship. They might be the number-one factor in the collapse of business deals. Here, the president didn't want to reveal his physical problems, so he chose to ignore them — a the cost of losing a potential client. When any problem recurs, decide ahead of time how to manage it. This prevents unnecessary surprises during sales calls.

Tradeshow Travesty
Thoughts on Napoleon

I LOVE TRADESHOWS! Of course, I collect sales horror stories, and tradeshows are a superb source. The observation of poor-performing, unprofessional sales reps is great entertainment to me. I might go so far as to equate a tradeshow visit with a Disneyland trip. Napoleons show up in great numbers at tradeshows. They fill exhibit booths (and their heads) with the attitude that customers are finally coming to them, so they get a couple days off from begging for business and indulge in a little role reversal — the prospects are actually coming to them for a change.

Because of this, an element of laziness seems to accompany tradeshow exhibiting. I've always believed that many of these salespeople were just hoping to get "discovered" by good customers. They leave their selling skills at home and expect the visitors to walk up, introduce themselves, and throw money at them.

I used to run an executive search firm. Where did I get to preview sales candidates most easily? At the salesperson's happy hunting grounds — tradeshows.

Unfortunately, "happy hunting grounds" has another meaning — the place where people go when they die. And sales reps die at tradeshows all day long.

They are acting like carnival barkers: they shout and wave brochures at passersby, hoping that you'll stop and play with them.

Selling in a booth is very different from selling in the field. Actually, it's more about generating leads than about closing sales. Most shows aren't for selling, but for visiting old clients and qualifying new prospects. Either way, most tradeshows are full of horrible sales practices. I'm tempted to offer proof of my feelings: to reinforce the fact that poor selling is going on, I'd love to take a video recorder and shoot people making the seven most common mistakes:

1. They are *sitting* in booths! There's a fine welcome for the prospect. The salesperson grunts as he or she pushes out of the seat, angry at the interruption of their rest and relaxation away from the office. I think most of the sitters are non-salespeople who get wrangled into working the show. The others are probably reps who partied a bit too late the night before.

2. They are standing behind "barriers." Some booths are simply designed wrong. Is selling about building walls, or is it about breaking them down or going around them? If, on an ideal sales call, you want to sit next to a prospect rather than having a desk between you, why would you design a sales environment that sends the wrong message to thousands of tradeshow visitors? One of us must cross over into the other's territory before anything good happens. Remove all barriers. Get out from behind the chair, table, display case, whatever. Just get nose to nose with your prospects.

3. They are acting like carnival barkers: they shout and wave brochures at passersby, hoping that you'll stop and play with them. 'Nuff said, you've been there, seen that.

4. They ask, "Can I help you?" A basic premise in selling is never to ask a question that can be answered by the word *no*. This is a rookie mistake in retail stores. You want to ask a unique opening question that puts the visitor at ease, like "What unusual things have you seen at the show that interest you?" Notice that this is an open-ended question that invites conversation. Better yet, ask a

question that might qualify the visitor, thereby determining whether you should invest talk time with him or her (see #6 below).

5. They shouldn't be working the show, someone else in the company should be. Many booth workers are assistants or administrative people who don't understand the sales process. A few years back, I was setting up a company's sales structure (designing campaigns and hiring manufacturer's reps) for an invention that would be introduced at the Consumer Electronics Show in Las Vegas. This is the biggest tradeshow in the country. Whom did the owners want to have in the booth? Good-looking women (who were, of course, acquaintances, not sales reps). My disgust took the form of sarcasm. "Right, you're going to Las Vegas; good-looking women will really stand out." A week before the show I got the call to help out. Someone had come to their senses: the women were out and sales pros were in. Put your best people in the booths. Let the rookies spend time observing the pros before they begin to "work" the crowd.

6. They don't understand how many show visitors are time wasters. These people have no intention of doing business with you, but they love to chat and they love whatever you're giving away (Snickers bars get lots of traffic, a bowl of shelled peanuts does not). This problem really is a qualifying issue. How quickly can you assess the value of a visitor before investing too much talk time? Back to Las Vegas. When visitors came to our booth, I asked the qualifying question, "Would you see yourself ordering at least a thousand of these?" When the president of the company — an inventor, not a salesperson — heard this, he became extremely upset with me. He felt that I was driving away smaller potential customers. He didn't realize that I was screening out time wasters. The serious small prospects will still want to talk, regardless of minimum order size. That was the president's lesson of the day: Qualify before presenting. And isn't that what learning a lesson is about? Often, it means you've experienced something that didn't make sense at first, then the little light bulb went on and you mumbled, "Aha!" This is a very profitable tradeshow lesson to learn: Qualify first, present later. By the way, you might not realize how many time wasters there really are. After years of attending every imaginable show (from both sides of the booth), I was asked to write a book for retirement-aged seniors,

describing how to attend tradeshows as a hobby! The book was to identify what shows would be the most fun, tell how to get in, and list all the interesting giveaways one could collect. A percentage of show attendees are there simply for the fun of it. They're out there, and they'll keep you from the visitor who has money for you, but can't get your attention while you chat with Auntie Jane.

7. They follow up too late to have an impact, or they never follow up. I just received correspondence from some companies I met *four months earlier* at a show in Chicago. The phone calls were identical. Everyone was surprised and a little hurt that I didn't remember them. After all, we practically became blood brothers when we met (they were getting ready for the happy hunting grounds). If you don't follow up with an immediate mailing, you might as well take your Las Vegas tradeshow money to the gaming tables and skip the investment in an exhibit.

These are seven basic fixable mistakes I see at tradeshows every time I attend. Identifying them is the first step in preventing them. Does your organization spend time and money on the tradeshow circuit? It would be wise to plan for what you want to accomplish and what you want to avoid.

Remember that video recorder I'm bringing to the show to shoot bad salespeople (I like how that sounds)? You're probably wondering what I'm going to do with that tape? I'll be making copies to send to the guy in each company who cut the check for the tradeshow expenses. I hope your CFO isn't on my list.

Good hunting,
Dan

One-upmanship Game Goes South

A car salesman reveals one of his bad days

IT WAS JANUARY IN WISCONSIN and absolutely freezing cold outside. A potential buyer drove to the front of the lot and got out to look at cars. I was the youngest sales guy on the floor, and it was my turn. So, I put on my jacket, which wasn't quite warm enough, and walked the cold seventy yards from the showroom to where the guy was looking into the windows of our used Cadillacs.

"I know exactly which year, make, and model of used car I want," the prospect said.

We hate this type. You really want to sell what's on the lot. And, of course, the car he wanted wasn't here. So basically, it's no sale, since this type never changes his mind. I'll show this guy, I thought.

"Would you wait just a minute, please?" I asked. "I have something for you." I sauntered back to the showroom and got razzed by the older guys. They did think what I was about to do was funny, though.

In the cold, I walked back to this guy and handed him a pencil with the dealer name and phone number on it. "This is for you. You can call another time to see if your car has been taken in trade." I tried to keep the smirk off my face. He had stood in the cold, waiting for a pencil! You get jerked around so much in this business; it's nice to get them back for a change.

The guy looked at me for a brief moment. He said, "Thanks! Could I have another one of these for my wife?"

Crap! What could I do? I walked all the way back to the showroom for another pencil and got ripped by the other reps. It was going to take me weeks to live down losing this one-upmanship game.

DON'T PLAY GAMES WITH PROSPECTS, however badly you think they qualify for that treatment. You never know what word of mouth could do to hurt you in the community. Instead, how about asking a question, like, "It's great that you know exactly what you want. Most people don't. Is there any circumstance under which you might consider another vehicle?" The answer is invariably yes, and you have a second chance to sell. Try out a version of this question in your next call when someone has already made up his or her mind. You could find that the conversation takes a positive turn toward the close.

You Probably Don't Know this Woman, but...

Philippe describes a rough day but manages to put a bad finish to it

I WORKED AS A SALES REP setting up promotional displays in stores. One very long, hot day I had nothing but problems: the stock hadn't arrived on time, space was not available — everything that could have gone wrong did. I finally managed to finish this particular store just as they were closing. It had been a fourteen-hour workday and all I wanted was out. As they locked the door, in walks a woman insisting that she see the department manager. Although not part of store staff, I tried to reason with her, telling her how busy Joe was. She insisted I get him.

I was mad as hell. I crashed into the back office and, in a loud voice, told him, "Some big fat old battle-ax just waddled into aisle seven demanding to see you."

She was his mother. I lost the account.

As THE SAYING GOES, it was the straw that broke the camel's back. What we need are stronger backs. Philippe has just learned the value of always maintaining one's composure and professional attitude when around clients. A public display of anger has no place in a sales professional's life. I'd suggest, at times like this, that Philippe close himself in a bathroom stall and let it all out.

Losing Face (and the Sale) Japanese-Style

 Mark humbly describes his humiliation selling consumer electronics to a major retailer

AFTER YEARS OF PURSUIT, I finally received a verbal commitment from my largest retail prospect, who was to buy more than $1.5 million in product over four months. My contact asked me to come to his office in early August to pick up the purchase orders.

I told my boss the good news. He told his Japanese counterpart, who told his boss in Japan. My boss told me he would meet me at the airport the day before the big order. To my surprise, he had his Japanese counterpart with him. On top of that, *his* boss had come over from Japan for the big event!

We went to dinner that night, and the big boss from Japan gave me a gift to show his appreciation for my efforts. They were cookies made by his mother. He also gave me a gift from the Japanese plant manager because, in his words, "You very famous in Japan."

The next day, at the retailer's headquarters, the buyer asked to see me alone before our group meeting. He sat me down and told me that, as a result of second-quarter results that had come in that morning, he'd been ordered not to add any new vendors and to reduce inventory levels. He then stood up and shook my hand, saying he had another meeting to go to and would not be able to see the other visitors. I was left to deliver this incredible news myself.

When I told the entourage in the lobby, the Japanese counterpart to my national sales manager refused to leave the building until he got an audience with the buyer. When I contacted his secretary, she ushered us in to the lunchroom and told us we might have to wait a long time. She came back to get us three hours later, and we met with the buyer.

I learned something about tenacity from that Japanese manager. He begged, pleaded, and cajoled the buyer, almost to the point of crying. But of course the buyer said his hands were tied and there was nothing he could do. To frustrate me further, my cell phone had been stolen from our rented car.

From this experience I learned never to count my chickens before they've hatched. Even though I had confirmed the appointment with the buyer only days before — and he confirmed his commitment to the deal — there was no way to tell that I was about to be ambushed by his company's terrible second-quarter results. I now never believe an order is real until it's signed, sealed, and delivered.

POSTMORTEM

A GREAT MANY EGOS contributed to this embarrassing situation. Perhaps Mark should have kept quiet until he had the agreement in hand. Certainly, his American sales manager should have refrained from contacting other key management figures. Also, the Japanese manager was afraid of losing face when he returned home empty-handed after telling everyone of their impending success, so his ego prompted him to beg for the sale. We've all counted on deals that fell through. This experience should teach us that it's a lot more fun to walk into the office with a signed contract, and celebrate, than to walk your management back to the plane with neither. Report your progress only as your job requires. Otherwise, limit expressing your hopes to your close circle of friends and family.

Sales Manager Earns Life Sentence in Voice Mail Jail

Terri and her boss deliver a malicious message

MY SALES MANAGER AND I had a full day ahead of us: a three-hour drive to deliver several one- to two-hour presentations for our specialty printing services, and a return trip. We began our day anticipating the acquisition of new business.

The town we were driving to offered us an intriguing opportunity. We're accustomed to calling on the Chicago metropolitan area, and the market for what we sell there is becoming saturated. This was a small town, which was probably not "hit on" like our regular territory. There were three large manufacturing plants using the type of products we sell.

We arrived in town and proceeded to our first two appointments. We excitedly landed at our third — and largest — prospect's office around two o'clock. We entered the lobby, walked up to the receptionist, and announced our arrival. The surprised receptionist informed us that our contact had taken the day off! I politely told her I would call him tomorrow, and quickly hustled my sales manager out of the lobby before his simmering temper erupted like a volcano. He is very protective of his salespeople's time, and has previously vocalized his displeasure in the lobby of a company after being "stood up."

We got back into the car, started driving out of the parking lot, and, after a bit of venting, decided our next step would be to call the prospect's office and leave a voicemail saying we'd been there and would reschedule an appointment. This call was made on my sales manager's cell phone using the speakerphone feature.

After I left the message, my sales manager and I both began to rant again, using some not-so-choice language and graphic detail. This went on for some thirty seconds, and then we heard a beep. We realized at that moment, half a minute too late, that our entire

91

conversation had been recorded on the prospect's voicemail!

There was absolutely nothing we could do to retrieve our stupid blunder. After two weeks, I called the prospect, acting like nothing happened, to reschedule our appointment.

That was three years ago, and he still won't take my call!

Because of the size of the opportunity, every time a new salesperson starts, the company makes the "rookie" call to try for an appointment. To this day, no one has been successful. I guess we just have to wait till that buyer with the red-hot ears leaves that firm!

 POSTMORTEM

AH, TECHNOLOGY, HOW IT CAN help or hurt us. Terri had a little button — a half-inch detonator — blow up her chances for a sale. Looking back, it's always easy to give perfect advice. But what if she had chosen not to succumb to the strong influence of her Napoleon-like manager? What if she had just offered some kind thoughts on why the buyer wasn't in that day? She could have gone back to the buyer and said something like, "Hey, my manager was really upset about not seeing you. But I know things happen and that you had some personal or business concerns that were probably quite important at the time. I'd like to come back, but I won't bring him with me." Then she could close for the appointment. Would she have had another shot at the buyer when she called? Most likely, yes — a better shot than the one a Napoleon complex gave her. One last thought on technology: I really believe that if electricity hadn't been invented, we'd all be watching TV by candlelight.

Retail Rant Wrecks Relationship

*Deb discloses the nightmare
that still haunts her
lonely bank account*

MY BIGGEST SALES/SERVICE NIGHTMARE was the day I wanted to crawl into the nearest hole and disappear. You know when you're having one of those really bad days, when everything anyone says to you is upsetting? I was having one of those days.

As a retail storeowner for fifteen years, I understood the importance of excellent customer service — otherwise there are no sales. I always strive to offer customer service that's above and beyond my competitors' — especially to the top 20 percent, my best and most valuable patrons.

On this day, my sales associate came into my office with a belt that had fallen apart. Looking at the belt, I knew it was old inventory and had been purchased some time ago. I yelled, "What do these people think, that we guarantee things for life? This is ridiculous! Tell them that there is *no way* we're going to do anything about it. That's final!"

My sales associate responded, "But, Deb, she's Mrs. B." Oops — Mrs. B. was one of my very best customers. I also didn't realize that the back door was open, and every customer in the rear of the store could hear my outrage. Of those customers, Mrs. B. was nearest, standing right outside of the doorway.

After realizing this grave error, in frustration (and disgust with myself), I came out to make amends with my valued customer. Trying to cover up my rudeness, I did the best I could to offer solutions to the problem and have the belt replaced. Every moment, I felt like I wanted to die of embarrassment.

Months went by, and no more Mrs. B. She never returned to my store. I sent out a letter of apology, made phone calls, and sent a nice gift, but my dear customer didn't come back, not even to pick up the replacement belt. She was gone forever. That bad day cost me tens of thousands of dollars in lost sales. This was a woman who bought expensive items for herself as well as for many of her friends. Talk about kicking yourself in the butt — I still can't sit down.

 POSTMORTEM

DO YOU EVER WONDER why there's so much news about the impact of anger on relationships? Co-workers attack their colleagues, spouses strike their loved ones, and people even get angry with themselves. Deb is irritated with her customer and, later, herself. Here is a word that will lighten your heart and smooth the relational paths of your life: *grace*. Give grace to others while you're in the process of finding out the real story. If Mrs. B. had purchased the belt two years ago and just begun to wear it, her return might be considered a legitimate product problem. Try first giving others the benefit of the doubt. And give yourself a break as well. The sooner we forgive ourselves and move on, the faster we will recover from the mental and physical ulcers with which we saddle ourselves.

E-mailing The Enemy

Heidi recalls a moment when her audience was bigger than expected

WHILE CONTRACTING as a Fortune 500 systems analyst in a specialized field, a shady contract broker stiffed me out of sixteen thousand dollars of revenue from a GM contract. It was whispered later by others who also had been cheated that he had been jailed on drug charges shortly after.

To my astonishment, some months after hearing this, I received an email from this crook, addressed to "My Business Clients." The message proudly announced his return to the industry and provided his new email address.

I was still very angry at his having cheated me. I couldn't believe that he had the nerve to keep me on his email list. I did something I'd never done: I wrote in a blind rage, "Go back to jail where you belong and take me off your mailing list!" I hit send without a second's hesitation.

An instant later, I was surprised to find my own message was back in my inbox. And just as suddenly, horror washed over me as I realized that this idiot had not written directly to me; instead, he had written to an industry list-serve consisting of hundreds of our mutual clients and consultants in our specialized field. My reply to him had been forwarded back to every one of them. I had just sent a very unprofessional flame-mail to my entire marketplace!

It's been over two years since I took this rash, impulsive action, and my face still turns red when I think of it. The scope and stupidity of my unprofessional conduct looms over me. I could very well have been sued for libel. This event certainly accelerated the career change I was undergoing. I never worked in that specialized field again. I learned never to communicate while still in the red haze of anger.

POSTMORTEM

TECHNOLOGY STRIKES AGAIN: another little button [SEND] clicked a big chunk out of Heidi's reputation. Like great athletes who get angry, great business professionals also turn that emotion inward and avoid the number-one sin that Napoleons commit. Don't wear your rage overtly; use it to motivate you to greater things. Heidi knew what she did wrong, but what she might not have known was that each time she explodes, it becomes easier to get angrier. The cycle grows bigger and faster. Keep cool and you'll keep your clients — and your friends, too.

The Ghost of Vince Lombardi

The Corporate Curmudgeon, Dale Dauten, shares how a flaw of the Sales Napoleon, a high-flying attitude, can undermine your performance.

---

*Say you really, really want to climb Mt Everest.
And so you go over there with the perfect attitude,
with all the grit and determination in the world,
but without knowledge, and what's going to happen?
You end up as Mrs. Paul's Frozen Optimist Sticks.*

The ghost of Vince Lombardi stopped by my office yesterday. That's right. He still had the cigar. (Turns out that Heaven doesn't have a *No Smoking* section — they're very conservative about their liberalism up there.) Anyway, here's what he said:

"Look, I don't have much time, 'cause I got to get back to my squad. We got a game against a team from the Dark Side and, you know how it is, they get most of talent down there. But I stopped in because I want to clear something up. All the time I hear people quote me, usually that business about 'Winning isn't the most important thing, it's the only thing.' Well, yeah, I said it. And that's why we need to talk. Lots of people look at my career and conclude that all you need to win is the right attitude. They think that if you want to win badly enough, you'll win, so they go around working at wanting. Bunk!

"Say you really, really want to climb Mt Everest. So you go over there with the perfect attitude, with all the grit and determination in the world, but without knowledge, and what's going to happen? You end up as Mrs. Paul's Frozen Optimist Sticks.

"When I got the Green Bay job, the Packers had just gone 1-10-1. And I said to the press, 'I have never been on a losing team and I don't intend to start now.' That wasn't braggadocio, it was a message to the players. They had to believe in me. You're not a leader till you have followers.

"And then I didn't just come in and start hollering, I started innovating. Yes, we had the toughest training of any team. We had the most intense practices. I wanted the games to be easier than practice. But what I want to get across is, we didn't just wish hard and try hard, we innovated. We invented the sweep, we invented new blocking schemes, and we were the first team to "read" defenses. We brought the passing game to the NFL. The upshot was that we were better prepared than the other guys. We had better players because we did a better job of educating them and training them. We had better plays. We didn't just *want* to win, we figured out *how* to win.

"Look at the great coaches and you'll see all kinds of personalities. They called John McGraw, who was the greatest baseball manager ever, 'Little Napoleon.' OK. But he invented the drag bunt, the double steal, the relief pitcher, and a lot of other stuff. Innovative dictators win.

"But guess what? Innovative saints win, too. Just picture John Wooden sitting on the sidelines, completely unemotional. The guy looked bored, for heaven's sake. He won because he developed the people around him. Every parent wanted his or her kid to play for him. Of course, being a saint will get you into heaven, but it won't save your job if you lose. He had the best-prepared players in the game. You know — and this amazed even me — he used to say, 'No player is better than his feet.' And he didn't just practice footwork; he actually had a class every season on how to put on socks. Yeah, socks.

"That reminds me of John Madden. Now there's a guy I should recruit for my assistant. I wonder what his cholesterol is? Anyway, I remember playing against Madden's Raiders in Super Bowl II. One of the turning points in that game was when their guy fumbled a punt and we recovered. Madden was sharp enough to figure out that our punter was left-footed, so the ball turned funny. And after that, whenever the Raiders were playing a team with a left-footed kicker, he'd bring in a guy who kicked that way to practice against. You win in practice.

"Well, I got to get back. I just wanted to make sure everybody understands how I feel. Don't worry about being great; worry about being better. Don't just try hard; innovate hard. If you want to motivate people, don't give them a great speech; give them great tools, great preparation, and great products. And then give them the credit, knowing that it's one thing you get more of the more you give away. And remember this: first find the daylight and then run for it."

Dale Dauten is a nationally syndicated columnist, author, and speaker. Dale's columns, *The Corporate Curmudgeon* and *Kate and Dale Talk Jobs*, appear in more than a hundred newspapers nationwide. Dale's most recent books include *The Gifted Boss* and *The Max Strategy*. Find him at www.dauten.com.

Sales Quotes to Toss Around the Office

THE BUYER'S CARROT

He promised me earrings, but he only pierced my ears.

— Arabian saying.

THE PROSPECTS' #1 JUKEBOX CHOICE

If the Phone Doesn't Ring, It's Me.

— Song title by Jimmy Buffet

AN UNSPOKEN RESPONSE TO THE MANAGER

Be respectful to your superiors, if you have any.

— Mark Twain

BAD LUCK FOR A BAD REP

Psychics will lead dogs to your body.

— Sales rep's fortune cookie message.

THE ROOKIE SALESPERSON'S DREAM

"Son, if you really want something in this life, you have to work for it. Now quiet! They're about to announce the lottery numbers."

— Homer Simpson

SONG OF THE SALES CALL

Maybe if we think and wish and hope and pray it might come true.

—"Wouldn't It Be Nice" by the Beach Boys

SUPER SELLING SYSTEM CREDO

George Robson, race driver, after winning the 1946 Indianapolis 500: All I had to do was keep turning left.

A EULOGY TO A LOUSY SALES MANAGER

The dead sales rep requested in his will that his body be cremated and ten percent of his ashes thrown in his sales manager's face.

Sales Maverick

Part Four

Sales Maverick

SALES MAVERICKS can be identified by their rebellious spirit. They are also a source of nightmares for sales managers and entrepreneurs. You can distinguish Mavericks because they:

Handle sales calls by winging it
Believe that salespeople are born, but rarely made
Will not learn or apply a system to their selling life

This rebellious "system fighter" rarely plans ahead of time what to say during the sales process. Because they also show plenty of ego, lost sales are always the fault of a potential client, who was dumb or not open to ideas that would make that prospect's life easier. There is, of course, no fault on the maverick's part, since their instincts are so good that they always handle a prospect perfectly. The maverick hurts sales management and company owners in several ways: They can wreck sales projections by mixing outstanding performance with wildly fluctuating failure. They damage sales team morale because they don't believe in the team concept. They don't take criticism well. However, this person's problem is not his or her ego. It is another concern.

Herein lies the root of the trouble with Sales Mavericks, who are always winging it:

They don't use a selling system.

Calling Card Company
Can't Clinch Client

*Tom rants that he's
ruined by a selfish buyer*

OUR COMPANY SELLS a new phone calling card that has users answer a survey before they get to use the free minutes. We presented to a major insurance company that was looking to determine patient satisfaction at a local hospital. It was going to be an easy sale. The current surveys were filled out and processed by hand. The results from their surveys were eventually compiled and made available — after about twelve months. Year-old information is as worthless as year-old milk. Also, only 12–15 percent of the patients filled out the forms.

Our surveys were totally automated by phone, and results were available in a week. Also, we typically get 40–50 percent of the patients to do the survey. We could blow away the old results and help the hospital respond very quickly to problems — before they got out of control.

The key decision-makers really liked it for all the right reasons: no paperwork to handle, benefit to patient for answering questions, quick analysis of patient treatment, and so on. On top of that, several medical groups were already using our method, so it wasn't a risky decision.

This was before we met the operations manager, who had six people processing all the paper forms. Letting those people go would cut three hundred thousand dollars out of her budget. She dug in her heels and refused to implement anything new.

I watched a hundred-thousand-dollar sale evaporate. I was disgusted and angry about it.

I learned that there are people who will protect their castle, even when living in castles today makes no sense.

MAVERICK TOM wasn't using a system, or he would have known that four buyer types exist in a complex sale. In *The New Strategic Selling*, Miller & Heiman identify them as Coach, User, Technical, and Economic. Note and memorize the CUTE acronym. The Coach gets you in the door. The User works with your solution every day. The Technical person sees that your solution coincides with their computers or internal systems. The Economic buyer writes your check. The User is the one who buried Tom. If the user will not implement your solution, you have a disaster on hand — especially if you sold the account and they never completely implement your product or service. Here's what you need to do: Develop four separate approaches to solve the problems of each of these four buyers. Present differently to each based on their unique needs. What motivates each person in his or her role at the company? See that you present and discuss critical concerns for each individual. You'll honor their uniqueness, and gain the support you need to close your sale — from all the players on the field.

I Just Knew There Was a Question I Forgot to Ask

Dan divulges a magazine deal that folds fast

JANE HAD THREE THINGS GOING FOR HER. She was a great salesperson, great looking, and her husband pitched for the Boston Red Sox. If you can't start a good conversation trying to place this woman into a sales job, you don't deserve to be in selling.

The worst problem in the search business is that most companies won't pay fees for salespeople. They can run an ad in the paper and get hundreds of responses. Why spend twelve thousand dollars on my services? So I was greatly relieved when a gentlemen who published a magazine agreed to pay my fee if he hired Jane. I set up the interview.

Jane was supposed to call me immediately after the meeting, but an excited magazine owner called me first, and spoke the words a recruiter lives to hear: "I love her. She's perfect for the job. I'll pay her asking salary."

I told him that I'd call him as soon as I got her feedback on the interview.

"*I can't believe you sent me there!*" she screamed into the phone. It was a pornography magazine.

I'd had no idea. The title of the publication didn't give a hint. Jane was very cool about it. We had some good laughs later, but it was nothing compared to the laughs in the Red Sox clubhouse when the story worked its way over there.

I learned to ask more questions to determine exactly what my prospects need help with.

POSTMORTEM

HERE'S WHAT REALLY happened to Dan: he hadn't learned to ask all the critical questions he needed to ask before offering a solution to the prospect's problem. Every salesperson knows that in his or her finite universe, certain things stay the same. Specific key issues must always be covered during the discovery stages of the sales process. Dan missed some questions that should have been built into his selling system. He didn't ask what type of customer the magazine targets, nor did he request a demographic description of its market. He would have found out two things: 1) Jane might have immediately said no to the interview, and, 2) He could have targeted a salesperson who calls on that target market already, providing a perfect potential solution to his prospect's need. Create a list of all the questions you should ask a prospect, and get them answered before offering your solution.

Sales Guy Out of Joint

Marvin needed to hire a sales professional for his film production agency

HE WAS A GOOD CANDIDATE, with a three-year gap in his employment history. His only child had been killed in a car accident, so, devastated, he went to work at a chemical plant outside the country. He wanted to hide from the world, so he stopped selling. I checked with a former employer. He was reserved, but said the guy was a good salesman and would do well.

After the new guy came aboard, equipment began to disappear, and a locked file cabinet was jimmied open. The big tip-off was when a young woman called, furious. She'd gone to bed with him — since he'd promised her a role in a movie.

We make industrial films!

Upon investigation, it was discovered that our man had never had a child. Those three years were spent in prison.

I called the former employer and asked, "Why didn't you warn me?" He was afraid of the guy! It was safer to lie to me than to have the ex-convict mad at him.

I learned to do a much better job checking out my potential employees after that.

 **POSTMORTEM**

MARVIN THE MAVERICK didn't have a system in place for sales hires. He winged it and got a tough lesson. By not thoroughly addressing all the steps of hiring a sales rep, he paid more than a wasted salary; he paid with his reputation. Today, it's even harder to do reference checks, in that former employers fear liability from making any negative comments about ex-employees. Get professional direction on what language to use when phoning references. Be consistent and systematic about your hiring procedures. Talk to a local search firm or contact the Society for Human Resource Management at http://www.shrm.org or (703) 548-3440.

Psychic's Sale Vanishes

Ginny swears she was stiffed by ... Death

I OWN AN OPTICAL SHOP and had an interesting sale last month. A psychic came in to buy two pairs of eyeglasses and get an eye exam. She picked out her frames and we discussed all of her options. She got the exam and I wrote up the sale. The total was $395.44.

She pulled out a credit card. I ran it and it was declined. She handed me another; it was declined. Finding this humorous, she tried four more cards. Then she said she would just write me a check. I thought the worst, but got all of her information and told her it would be several days before the glasses would be ready. I purposely waited eight business days to make sure the check was good. I called her to come pick them up. She left happy and I thanked her for her business.

The next day her check was withdrawn out of my account. She had stopped payment on it. I was furious! I called her and told her this was fraud and I would go to the fullest extent to get the money back. She said she thought it was buy one-get one free. I told her we don't offer that because our pricing is so reasonable. Even if we did, she had no right to pick up the glasses and cancel the check. She agreed to make it good and said she would be in the next day to pay it.

I waited a week and sent a certified letter that came back refused. So I went to the police station and spent three hours getting a warrant for her arrest. I thought that since she was psychic, she would realize I was going to have her arrested. That night, when reading the newspaper, I read something very disturbing: her obituary. She had died three days earlier! I have spent every day checking with

Probate Court and as of today she has no estate. My lesson in this sale: If the patient is psychic, *get cash!*

 POSTMORTEM

HERE IS A PERFECT PROBLEM that defines the need to put a system into place for managing your selling and your entire business. A working, proven system is why franchises are far more successful than independent startups (you are three times more likely to fail as an independent business). In a system, most decisions are pre-made. You're never confused about how to handle a given situation. In fact, there should be a written manual dictating how to act, so that whatever situation occurs, a response is already in place. If prospect does action A, entrepreneur (salesperson) responds with B. If action X, then respond with action Y. Ginny needed to ignore her desire to close a sale, and trust her instinct to protect her bank account. If someone gives you six credit cards that don't work, cash might be the only option. I described this problem to an entrepreneur who was previously an accountant. He said that if Ginny had been an accountant, she would have handled this coldly from a perspective that first considers financial wisdom. You only take cash from high-risk customers. Decide ahead of time how to deal with your fairly common business scenarios. It's a huge relief not to be creative on the fly. Use your written manual and go "by the book." You might sell less, but you'll buy fewer headaches, too.

The Perfect Pitch

*A tale for prospects
who crash and burn*

LIEUTENANT MILLER WAS ASSIGNED to the Air Force enlistment center, where he advised new recruits about their government benefits, especially their insurance.

Before long, Captain Smith noticed that Lieutenant Miller had a near-100-percent record for insurance sales. Everyone Miller spoke to bought additional coverage. This had never happened before. Rather than ask about it, the captain stood in the back of the room and listened to Miller's sales pitch.

Miler explained the basics of the insurance to the new recruits, and then said, "If you have U.S. armed services insurance and go into battle and are killed, the government has to pay a quarter-million dollars to your beneficiaries. If you don't have this additional insurance, and you go into battle and get killed, the government only has to pay a maximum of six thousand."

"Now," he concluded, "which bunch do you think they're going to send into battle first?"

POSTMORTEM

OKAY, THAT'S AN OLD JOKE, but it proves an excellent point. If you understand the real implications of your prospect's choices, you'll close a ton more sales than you do now. Real implications mean the ultimate, personal impact of those choices to the buyer. In this story, the prospect was led to believe that he was buying safety from death. Discover what your prospect fears, and sell to protect that buyer's future. Your new clients will love you for protecting them. The key here is how interestingly Lt. Miller contrasts with the Sales Maverick. Miller's presentation is identical every time, so his results are consistent and outstanding. He's developed a system that wins for him. You can do the same.

Do Your Proposals Allow Prospects to Steal Your Brainpower?

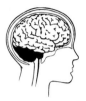

(Including the Top Ten List of reasons why a prospect demands a proposal)

Thoughts on the Maverick

PROPOSALS ARE THE FOUNDATION of business building for most salespeople. How many of us constantly invest precious sales time to draft a proposal, actually pouring years of experience and expertise into this written gamble at acquiring business? The Maverick spends lots of time proposing because he or she doesn't employ a qualifying system before designing these documents.

They give you their biggest smile and drain your brain of all its problem-solving knowledge before you understand their true intentions.

One reason most of us are so quick to accommodate potential clients is that we really do want to please people. Think of how ridiculous it would sound if you refused to provide materials to your prospect! So you and I are very likely to assume that a request for a proposal is a *yes* indicator. It reinforces our hope that we've just moved one step closer to closing the sale. There is, however, the prospect's perspective. If we don't understand what might really be going on with that request, we could spend endless hours creating and delivering documents for people who have no intention of buying our products or services. And here's why:

Prospects love free consulting. They give you their biggest smile and drain your brain of all its problem-solving knowledge before you understand their true intentions. And they love it even more in print than in person. If you don't have a strategy for dealing with proposal requests, you're at the mercy of every potential client. Over the past twenty years, I've analyzed many of the top sales training organizations. It's interesting to note that virtually all the great training systems have the wisdom to recognize and teach how critical it is for a salesperson *not* to give everyone proposals simply because they are requested. To help you understand the dangers of proposal writing, here's a list you'll learn from.

The Top Ten Reasons a Prospect Demands a Proposal (The impact to you is in parentheses)

10. They need to keep their current vendors honest *(what a surprise — you never had a prayer of getting the business)*

9. They want a fair range of prices for the type of service you offer *(thanks for the quote, the business is going to the prospect's brother-in-law, at just below your rate)*

8. They want to keep themselves up-to-date on the latest business processes and technologies *(thanks for the education, goodbye)*

7. They think your product or service simply sounds interesting *(but they have no intention of buying!)*

6. They need new and better ideas — to make their own changes *(thanks for your free consulting; that really hurts, doesn't it?)*

5. They just wonder how much it would cost *(wow, you're really expensive!)*

4. This request will get you off their back *(oops, you forgot to qualify the prospect, didn't you?)*

3. They can look good when they pass your information to the real decision-maker *(did you spend all that time with the wrong person?)*

2. They honestly need their problems solved *(too bad you don't know whom the other eight proposals are from, what they charge and maybe what they're saying about you)*

And the number one reason prospects make you pour your blood, sweat, and tears into a proposal:

1. A prospect can lie to a salesperson and still get into heaven!

Final Thoughts:

Preparing proposals can offer false hope to all sales pros. Do you really believe that everyone asking for a customized, written solution is ready to buy?

Please, please, stop wasting your time jumping through hoops to design proposals for everyone that nods his head or grunts into your telephone. *Qualify first*, and then begin to work with your best potential clients. Your organization should have some criteria for what defines a good prospect. Use them, or immediately create your own to save yourself from sales heartbreak. If you don't quickly sort the good prospects from the time wasters, bad prospects can sabotage your income. Your expectations of who will buy from you will be inaccurate. One good method might be to charge a fee for a proposal. Obviously, a prospect who's not serious won't pay for it. If this works for you, implement it. However, your organization might not choose to use this strategy, so get a grip on what looks like a realistic buyer and craft your plan without giving away all your solutions.

The lesson here is that you need to set guidelines to determine which prospects are worth investing your time in proposal design. Otherwise, you'll waste lots of time showboating in print for prospects who have no intention of doing business with you. If you don't weed out the weeds, you'll have very little time to find, smell, and pick the flowers.

Salesman Discovers The Law Is Not On His Side

Darin details his dreadful experience selling for a law firm

THE TWO SEVENTY-YEAR-OLD attorneys wanted to grab a ton of business before they retired. That way, their prestigious law firm would sell for more money. Their plan was to offer their own "prepaid" legal services to Illinois companies that had more than two hundred employees.

The firm already had a prepaid program with some local unions, so they had a proven service to offer. I had received the marketing contract to expand their business. After identifying the decision-makers for their exact market, I began to contact the target companies for appointments.

When I secured my first sales call, a large group of auto dealerships, I asked one of the partners to go with me. Who would know the service better than he would?

The human resources director showed us into her office and had great news. She was the person who'd handled our legal services in her previous job at one of the unions! We were basically there to give her some details of the service and explain how much it would cost her. It was going to be one of the easiest sales I'd ever made.

"When I became a lawyer in 1955 ..." began the partner. And I knew I'd made a mistake. Forty minutes and four decades later, my "selling" partner finished. He'd contributed nothing of value to the meeting unless the HR director or I wanted a job as his biographer. I managed to salvage the rest of our time together, and we ended the meeting on a very upbeat note. She wanted the costs for six hundred employees and would immediately put it into their benefits program.

"Wow!" I said as we entered the elevator outside the company's headquarters. "We struck gold on the first sales call."

The attorney looked at me for several seconds and said, "I don't want them as customers."

I was stunned. "What do you mean?" I asked. The commission was worth eighteen thousand dollars to me each year the contract was in place.

"They're automotive people. You know—car salesmen, mechanics. I don't want to have those kinds of people as clients."

I looked at the guy in disgust. Attorneys! This potential client was not simply a $120,000-a year contract to the law firm. Since it was a monthly "subscription" service, typical business valuation practices made it worth ten times the gross amount — a whopping 1.2-million-dollar increase in the value of the law firm! Imagine getting a dozen or so similar clients over the next six months, then selling the firm for fifteen — twenty million dollars more than previously planned. It amazed me that they wouldn't just take the money and run. In other words, all of these clients were worth closing to jack up the sale value of their company.

Incredibly, the other lawyer agreed with his partner. I terminated the relationship immediately. My short-term retainer was nothing compared to what I could have earned. I now ask a lot more questions before I take on new clients.

POSTMORTEM

THIS IS AN UNUSUAL PROBLEM, because it happened after the hardest sale, the marketing contract, had been made. Darin made a simple mistake while "closing" the law firm to get his contract: he asked about the exact target markets of companies, but he didn't ask which companies to ignore. Because he wasn't following a system, Darin missed the "close after the close," meaning he didn't discover what might undo the sale. A safe way to phrase this would have been to ask, "Are there any circumstances under which you wouldn't work with one of the target market firms?" He might have gotten answers like, "No one who's a threat to our image" or, "Here's a list ..." When you've already closed a sale, remember to ask your new client what might change things. It's really the close after the close. You'll save yourself some surprises. Again, the lack of a simple list of questions, a piece of a system, sunk Darin's sale.

Sales Rep's Cell Is Not His Phone

Leon laments his jail time on a call

SEVERAL YEARS AGO, I was making a sales call on a county jail. I accompanied the woman who did the purchasing of janitorial supplies to the basement to check stock. Supplies for the jail were in a cage inside some kind of holding cell. No sooner had we opened the cage, than someone came to tell her of an important phone call.

As she left, I noticed a lonesome commode in the room, and suddenly felt the urge to "go." Knowing she had just left and would have to climb the stairs and then answer her call, I took advantage of the situation; I closed the door to the room and relieved myself.

Feeling confident that I had taken care of business in plenty of time, I reached for the handle to open the door.

Did you know that they don't put handles on the inside of cell doors?

Not panicking, and knowing that the lady would soon return, I proceeded to check the jail's stock. Time passed and the minutes got longer. They soon stretched into an hour, and panic did set in. As I looked for a means of escape, I spotted a broom. There was the answer — I would use it to bang out a signal on the ceiling. Grasping it firmly, I hit the ceiling with authority. The room reverberated with a little *tink!* What a lonesome sound that was as I hit the plate metal. Hitting, yelling, and banging did no good at all. I just was going to have to "do my time."

Approximately an hour and a half had gone by, when an embarrassed lady opened the door and apologized several times for forgetting me. While writing this, I realized that I no longer call on county jails. Why should I? I've done my time!

 **POSTMORTEM**

IF ANYONE EVER HAD A CHANCE to "guilt" a client into buying, this was it. But here's what really happened: Leon's sales call was interrupted by a phone call. This happens frequently in selling situations, though most salespeople aren't in jail when the call arrives. You've probably sat in front of prospects when they took a call. How important did you feel when that occurred? A Maverick feels that any situation that arises can be handled on the fly. A true sales pro anticipates trouble and addresses it before it crashes his or her sale. In a case like this, please get an agreement with prospects and clients that you will not be interrupted by anything short of an emergency. Get the agreement before the meeting, when you call to confirm or when you sit down to begin talking. Here's some language you might try: "Mr./Ms. Prospect, thanks for meeting with me today to handle this (describe serious issue or problem you can solve). Is this concern you've expressed important enough that we can avoid any distractions during our time together? How can we keep from being interrupted?" If you feel gutsy, ask that the assistant hold all but urgent calls. If you allow interruptions, you'll lose momentum and focus during a sales call. On your next appointment, try this language or something similar that you're comfortable with. Build this small step into your sales process today. Take the value of your problem-solving ability more seriously. Be a professional and expect others to respect your time as well as their own.

Dead Grandpa, Dead Deal

Dan details how his rookie realtor dug into a hole

THE NEW AGENT IN MY OFFICE was quite excited about showing his first listing to a well-qualified client.

In the real estate licensing class, we're taught that it's not a good idea for the owner to be in the home when it's being shown. But our new agent was confident of his skills, and when the owners requested that they be allowed to help with the showing, he agreed.

Afterward, he returned to the office a thoroughly beaten man.

"It was great at first," he said. "They loved the house and everything about it. The owners followed us everywhere as we toured the house, and the clients seemed to be totally sold. But we kept coming back to a beautiful little family room with a very expensive antique sofa. When the clients commented on the attractiveness of the sofa, the owner proudly replied, "Yep, that's where Grandpa died.""

The husband and wife both turned pale as baby powder, and stared first at the owner, then the sofa, then each other. Together they headed for the door. That was the end of the showing — and the end of the clients.

Our lesson? Pretty obvious, I'd say. Get the owners out of there!

POSTMORTEM

DAN'S AGENT FELL INTO A TRAP into which many rookies collapse. He tried to re-invent the wheel. The rookie should never have allowed the owners to be there. In any proven system, the greatest guarantee of success is to follow that system — religiously. Here we see the Maverick winging it again, thinking he could handle anything that popped up. The blame also lies with the manager, who should insist that no one make up his or her own rules. If you're an entrepreneur or salesperson, find a selling model that works, learn it, and then apply it consistently. It'll make your life easier, guaranteed.

Burn Money Hiring Sales Reps?

Corey buys selling lessons late in his career

AS THE VICE PRESIDENT OF SALES for a national title company, I spent a lot of time interviewing and hiring. So it was a great relief to find a headhunter who understood exactly the type of salespeople I wanted. He got me an area manager who was fantastic, and I gladly paid the $10,500 fee.

Four months later, I called the headhunter for help with a national accounts position. In two days, he had uncovered two outstanding candidates who began to fight for the job. They even knew each other. After I had hired one and sent the recruiter a check for $14,100, I found out why things went so quickly. The headhunter had called my area manager (the one he got for me) to ask for referrals for the opening! She had told him, "Call these guys, they're perfect fits for the position."

I couldn't decide whether to be mad at someone — maybe even myself — or disgusted that I'd spent fourteen grand of my budget. I could have asked my area manager for help and gotten my hire for nothing. When I called the recruiter, he said, "Well, you teach your salespeople to ask for referrals from their best client relationships, don't you?"

Our new hiring policy is to post jobs to employees first. We pay them a mere five hundred dollars for referrals we hire.

⚰ POSTMORTEM

COREY PAID FOURTEEN THOUSAND DOLLARS for a basic selling lesson: Ask for referrals! The recruiter nailed the real issue when he attributed success to asking for help. Tell everyone that you need help and you'll end up with many more options than you had when the problem arose. Do you ask for referrals as part of your selling process every day? It should be part of your selling method.

Another tactic: Join a referral or networking group in your area. The top international organization that forms and manages these groups is Business Network International. Find a location for your local meeting at www.bni.com. There's no cheaper way to make money.

How Valuable Is Your Autograph?

Sales manager Cathy talks about wasting a few vehicles' worth of profits

THE CUSTOMER WAS ONE of those really savvy guys. He'd done his homework and had all of our numbers: cost of the vehicle, markup on options, etc. When you're selling a car to this type, you just make sure you do the best you can. If he buys, you've moved another unit; if he doesn't, well, at least you didn't spend a ton of time negotiating over every little accessory.

We got him! He gave us a beautiful Maxima in trade. He was going to get financing from his bank, and wanted to do it without cash, using his tiny equity in the Maxima (and our discount) to swing the deal. To cover our butts, we had him fill out a finance form. You do that with everyone. Then, if they don't get their own money, they have to borrow through us — and we make more money on the deal from our lenders. He was an entertaining guy and, in the finance office, told us some car jokes that even we had never heard.

The guy drove his new Honda into the dealership three days later and asked for his Maxima back. Well, I had news for him. I walked him into the finance manager's office and explained that his car had been shipped to Kuwait. They still needed nice cars over there, since the war had destroyed everything. He said that his bank wanted him to have an additional twelve hundred dollars before they'd finance the vehicle. He wasn't going to spend more cash and just wanted to forget the deal.

With perfect timing, the finance manager pulled out the customer's paperwork and waved it around. "Sorry," my finance manager explained, "we have a signed contract and you'll have to use us. We can build the twelve hundred into the deal, it'll just cost you a slightly higher interest rate."

"What contract?" the guy said, genuine surprise on his face. It was handed to him and he turned it over. There at the bottom of the page was the signature line, still blank.

In all the fun we were having that day, it had never been completed. Of course, we had already sold the guy's car, so we had to eat the twelve hundred ourselves. We lost big money selling that car. Twelve hundred dollars is a huge amount over our profit margin on a slim deal. The owner really chewed me out over that one. Boy, did I learn to be a stickler for filling out forms after that.

POSTMORTEM

THIS REMINDS ME of the kind of scams that bank tellers are warned about, people switching bills and such. What's really awful is that the sale was not only lost, but sales manager Cathy lost real money on top of her mistake — she paid cash to sell her product! You can't survive long in business doing that. How did this all happen? The finance manager didn't follow his system. He missed a piece — a signature — and it cost the dealership money. Define your selling system and your process and focus on working them completely.

Cold Calling for Thirty Million Dollars

*Charles confesses that
he can't bank on his bank*

THE TOUGH THING about cold calling is, well, the cold calling. The great thing about cold calling is, sometimes you get really lucky. Sometimes your timing and a prospect's timing are perfectly aligned and a large sale results.

I was cold calling to sell retirement plans when I found a man who was unhappy with his organization's current plan. He was in the process of finding a new provider. He was also the president of one of the largest unions in my state, and the retirement plan in question had thirty million dollars in assets!

We met him in person several times and got along great. He recommended that we do a presentation to the union's thirteen-member state board. Only one other firm was competing for the business. Our recommendation was that we handle the investments, and that a local bank handle the administration. We thought that by keeping the business in the community we increased our chances of landing the account.

On the day of the presentation, the other firm went first and we followed. As I talked about the investments, several board members nodded their heads. I thought we had the deal locked up. We then introduced a representative from the bank to briefly discuss administration of the plan. After his brief comments, we fielded several questions, which were all minor except the last one.

A board member asked, "Is it true your bank is building a new branch in a neighboring town and using non-union labor?"

The answer was yes. We lost the account by default.

The moral of the story: Be careful about whom you do business with jointly, or whom you refer to your clients.

 # POSTMORTEM

As GOOD AS REAL SALES PROS are at covering all the details, even the smallest items can sneak by undetected, and sink your ship as it's ready to sail. This story is important because it highlights the problems we have asking for referrals. Charles didn't have enough critical information about his referral partner and it cost him a thirty-million-dollar account. If you don't have intimate knowledge of the person or company you're partnering with, you risk *your* reputation when they fail to offer quality service or simply screw up a deal. So, know your "partners" well. Know them well enough to understand how they might close a deal or kill one. Only then can you proudly offer that partner as a solution for a prospect or client.

The Most Expensive Writers in the World

Proposal expert Tom Sant shows how the Sales Maverick's lack of a qualifying system means that they burn cash by drafting proposals for everyone.

If they're doing their own letters, proposals, and presentations, your salespeople are probably among the most expensive writers in the world. And to make matters worse, they're probably not very good at it, either. Typically, it takes a salesperson hours to write a proposal. That's time spent in front of a computer instead of a customer. What does this yearly investment cost?

Here are three ways to calculate the outrageous cost of a Maverick's many proposals:

Note: Insert your own figures into each calculation to find your "burn" rate. While this includes some simple mathematical calculations, the value of knowing what it costs to generate proposals is something you'll want to be aware of.

Salesperson Salary = $100,000

Hourly Salary Rate = $50

(Salary/2000 hours: 50 weeks   40 hours)

Hours Invested per Proposal = 12

Number of Proposals per Year = 10

Annual Quota per Salesperson = $1,000,000

Hourly Quota Rate = $500

(Quota/2000 hours: 50 weeks   40 hours)

Value of Proposal in Sales Dollars = $50,000

Your sales people are probably among the most expensive writers in the world. And to make matters worse, they're probably not very good at it, either.

1. Costs based on salary formula:
Hours Invested per Proposal   Number of Proposals per Year
Hourly Salary Rate: Calculation is 12   10 $50 = $6,000. Portion of salary burned yearly in proposal writing: six thousand dollars!

2. Costs based on sales quota formula:
Hours Invested per Proposal   Number of Proposals per Year
Hourly Quota Rate: Calculation is 12   10 $500 = $60,000
Portion of quota burned yearly in proposal writing: sixty thousand dollars!

3. Costs based on proposal value formula:
Value of Proposal in Sales Dollars / Hours Invested per Proposal = $4,167 per hour. Next: Hourly Rate by Proposal Value   Hours per Proposal   Number of Proposals per Year.
Calculation is 4,167   12   10 $50,000.
Portion of proposal value burned annually in proposal writing: more than a half-million dollars! *Other than Stephen King or John Grisham, nobody is making that kind of money writing!*

Tom Sant is the author of the book, *Persuasive Business Proposals.* Tom's company provides best-selling software to automate proposals, sales letters, and presentations.
Find him online at www.santcorp.com.

Miscellaneous Malpractice

Part Five

Miscellaneous Malpractice

The Dummies and the Dumbstruck

MANY OF THESE SELLING DISASTERS are funny because they center on completely unexpected events. We're often surprised by what a prospect does to us, or by what we do to ourselves. And like a good joke, the punch line comes from nowhere, but it really does make sense in a sick or sad sort of way.

So, let's stumble off into the woods like deer in the headlights, and laugh, and learn from the misfortune of our selling colleagues who've fallen before us.

Three-Ring-Circus Selling

 *Scott admits he's the ringmaster of this disaster*

IT WAS A HOT AUGUST DAY and we were about forty-five minutes early to demonstrate our data technology services. My partner and I decided to get a cold drink at the closest convenience store. I bought a super-large frozen cherry thing, and my partner got a lime-flavored one.

We drove back to the prospect's building and sat in the visitor's spot, mentally preparing, and drinking frozen pop. When we were ready to go, I looked over, and my partner's mouth, lips, teeth, and tongue were *bright green* — I mean really bright, like a clown's.

I grabbed the rearview mirror and flipped it toward my face. My features were *glowing red.*

We couldn't wash it off, wipe it off, or anything, so we went into the sales call looking like a couple of circus clowns. People actually laughed when we came in; we were never asked back.

POSTMORTEM

OBVIOUSLY, THINKING more carefully about one's actions just before a sales call is important. However, the psychological reason a call like this fails is that you can't gain rapport with a prospect if he or she is uncomfortable being sold by circus clowns. There's no hope for a rep who makes an unprofessional first impression on a prospect. I told this tale while speaking to the Chicago Chapter of Sales & Marketing Executives International, and received a smart suggestion for Scott: Bring some frozen drinks for the prospect, too — it might just save the sale.

Moving Earth to Sell In Chicago

Don remembers the colossal calamity of his tradeshow experience

IMAGINE A TRACTOR TIRE SO huge that four men — each six feet tall — could stand on one another's shoulders and be unable to touch the top of it. We manufactured earth-moving equipment that large. One of our big tradeshows each year is in Chicago, a strong union town. To show everything off, we had to ship our gigantic cranes and tractors in three rail cars to the train yard in Chicago. From there, the equipment would be moved over to the show floor, where visitors could gaze in amazement at our products.

There was one small problem, but it had existed for many years: We were not a union organization.

On this trip, the railroad cars disappeared.

Our sales team was in total panic. What were we going to do with a huge booth of … carpet? Someone contacted our ad agency, and giant cardboard mock-ups of the cranes and tractors were thrown together. They arrived just before the show opened. Those cardboard replicas were actually noticed better than the real thing. But we were still missing millions of dollars worth of equipment.

Somehow the strong unions in Chicago had decided to sabotage our non-union appearance. They did a great job of it. Our equipment was finally 'found' in the railroad yards — six months after the show ended!

We learned to send a human escort to accompany our machines.

 ## POSTMORTEM

DON WAS A VICTIM of industrial sabotage. How could he anticipate such a dramatic incident? We're never taught how to deal with "enemies," are we? Don't hide from potential danger. Flush it out and confront it. I recently bought a car and had seven days to return it. I did, on the evening of the seventh day. The sales manager was upset, until I asked him why nobody had called me during that time to see how things were going. The salesman had chosen to hide and hope that the sale would finish closing on its own. In Don's situation, he might have called the head of the local union and asked him to see that nothing embarrassing happened to his reputation or Don's equipment. Be proactive. Reactive people are always scrambling to fix things, often too late to save the sale.

When You Absolutely Have to Ruin Your Sale Overnight

Keith decides it's time to change sales managers

MY BOSS INSISTED on tailing along for the sales call of a lifetime. Our company located tax credits for major corporations, and I had landed an appointment with a Fortune 100 client who provided package delivery and pickup.

The sales call went better than we expected, and we left confident that we had earned their trust and business. As my manager dreamed about the commissions, we planned how to proceed.

"We need to lock them down immediately," he said as we returned to the office. I prepared the contracts and put them on his desk for approval.

The next day, I asked him if he'd had a chance to go over them. "I did better than that," he replied. "I've already sent them overnight to our new client."

Trouble was, he had overnighted the contracts to our package delivery client *using their main competitor.*

Needless to say, a furious company executive refused to sign the contract.

I learned the lesson: Always pay attention to the details. Never again will I let someone else "take care" of one of my customers.

POSTMORTEM

AND YOU THOUGHT SALES MANAGERS became bosses because they were great salespeople or deserved it. Keith later told me that his manager blamed him for not attending to the details! Of course, Keith wasn't around when the package was sent out, so he couldn't be faulted. Regardless of where blame is placed, the lesson is critical for selling professionals. Any little detail can make or break a deal. In the Old Testament, there's a small line — with big implications — that says, "... the little foxes spoil the vines." The phrase refers to small creatures that nibble away at the grapes before they can be harvested and generate profits. In essence, you won't get to enjoy the fruits of your labors if you don't watch out for the fine points of doing business professionally. Keith's real lesson? Nobody but Keith is responsible for his success. An old Arabic proverb says, "Trust Allah, but tie your camel." Don't let anyone intercept your sale on the way to success. You handle the details. Lean a bit toward perfectionism if you have to, and see that your success is a result of your attention to details.

Oprah Winfrey and the Easter Grass

Tom shares his sales call to kill for

OPRAH WINFREY WAS LOOKING for new inventions for an upcoming show. I knew we were perfect for this, since we had a telephone device that electronically blocked dialing out from the phone. There were lots of 900-line horror stories going around, like "Kid runs up $2000 bill while mom is at work."

We showed up at the studio and sat in a large waiting area with about a hundred and fifty other people. Like me, they were all here for the sales call of a lifetime: an appearance on Oprah could mean you were set for life. A crowd of fascinating people with strange devices milled about, just waiting for the chance to do a four-minute pitch to Oprah's producer.

After waiting four hours, I walked up to a couple who had an Easter basket sitting between them. "What do you have?" I asked. The woman spoke excitedly, either out of genuine passion for her product or out of a need to practice her pitch. "We have invented edible Easter grass for Easter baskets! Kids can eat the grass after finishing off their candy. It's even FDA approved — the same type of material as Gummi Bears ."

My mind jumped one simple step beyond their thinking, planning, and production process. "Well, that's pretty neat. But what if a kid thought *real* Easter grass was your candy and he ate it and choked on it. Couldn't *you* be sued?"

The man and woman looked at each other for a long moment. Then, without a word, they got up and walked out the studio door.

 POSTMORTEM

WOW! IMAGINE THE EMBARRASSMENT a major TV show might have experienced if they promoted this product and then a tragedy occurred. Taking a new item to market is very difficult. The inventors had a great idea, but probably didn't test it enough outside their circle of influence. A simple solution like a wild color might have made it a profitable product. A great idea from this story is the ingenuity of leveraging a company with a TV talk show or radio show appearance. Does that intrigue you? Design a press release that puts a unique spin on what you do, and start pitching producers. Contact the resource that helped put *Chicken Soup for the Soul* into radio and TV fame. *Radio-TV Interview Report* provides a list of contacts that you can mail or fax. See http://www.rtir.com or call Stephen Hall Harrison at 800-989-1400.

Memorable Lunch, Missed Sale

Jeff speaks of slipping up while selling his marketing services

I FLEW IN FROM CALIFORNIA for a lunch meeting with two conservative Midwest grocery executives. They were interested in developing the relationship and making use of our services. I brought along another consultant from our firm.

We picked up the clients and went to their favorite restaurant, a really chic downtown place. It was a rehabbed loft with funky furnishings, neon lights, and a wild menu. After we were seated, I excused myself to visit the men's room, which was just as wild as the rest of the place. The sink was a fountain-like structure in the middle of the room, with floor pedals to turn the water on. Paper towels hung from the ceiling.

After returning to the table, my consultant went to the men's room. Then the clients got up to go. The clients returned quickly, red-faced and laughing. The consultant came back and we had a normal business lunch, talking about some upcoming projects they wanted bids on. We dropped them off at their office and then flew home.

I called the clients the next day to get their feedback on the meeting; they told me that it went well, but they felt my buddy was a little weird. When I asked them to elaborate, they said, "Well, we walked into the men's room and he was standing on his tiptoes, peeing in the sink!" I couldn't control my laughter and told them that the offbeat furnishings were a bit confusing.

They never did engage us in any studies, and to this day I think they felt we were a bunch of weirdoes from California.

JEFF HAS TWO ISSUES to deal with here. First, after hearing the problem, don't be afraid to ask a question like this: "Wow, you probably have some concerns about doing business with someone like that, don't you?" It takes guts, but it can deflate the balloon of doubt floating overhead. Get the issues on the table. Conservative buyers still do business with weirdoes from California — if they need what you've got. Second, there's a great deal of energy invested in sales lunches. Think hard about doing these meals. Are they a good time investment? Possibly not, when you consider that most of the time isn't spent selling; it's spent using your money, or your company's, to do what everyone does daily — eat. The conversation might be more focused at your office or the prospect's, where time is more highly valued and respected. Save lunches for that rare close, or better yet, for a thank you to a new client or an existing one whom you really appreciate.

Headhunter Records
Dishonest Prospect

*Dan shows how his
sale slipped into oblivion*

I REMEMBER ZIG ZIGLAR'S IDEA about recording sales calls by hooking a tape recorder to the phone. It really helped in many ways. I stopped saying "uh," and I realized the value of scripting my calls ahead of time. Lots of phone sales guys I knew did this — even though it was considered illegal to tape a phone conversation without informing the other party.

I had a woman, Dawn, interviewing for the presidency of a small medical products firm. The company was from the Middle East and wanted to build its U.S. presence. The owner's personal assistant, a good friend of mine, had informed me of the job opening. Dawn was an ideal candidate and the meetings progressed well. I recorded all my conversations with the parties involved — just to keep a record of my experience.

Dawn was about to get hired when she shocked me with a call to say she wasn't taking the job. The owner had told her that he would pay her what she wanted, but he wanted to avoid paying my fee of twenty-four thousand dollars by having a sister company in New York hire her! No deal — she wouldn't work for someone whose ethics were so questionable.

"Who knows how he might treat me one day?"

I had it all on tape.

I was shocked and angry, and now it was my turn to do something dumb. I called the owner's personal assistant at home to tell her what kind of guy she was working for. I got her answering machine and left a detailed message.

She had it all on tape.

I took the call from an angry owner the next morning. My friend had brought her answering machine tape into work and played it for her boss, confronting him about his ethics!

Everyone lost: Dawn got no job; my friend got a new job; the medical products company got no president; and I lost a twenty-four-thousand-dollar fee.

What can I say that I learned? Sometimes you do all the right things. If someone is deceitful, they're unlikely to come out and inform you of that fact. You just have to hope that God gets even with them — soon.

☠ POSTMORTEM

MOST SALES FAILURES have underlying problems related to technique or attitude. Not here — sometimes you just get unlucky and hook up with a dishonest person. Robert Ringer's classic book, *Looking Out for Number One*, describes three types of buyers: There's the honest buyer. There's the buyer who's going to take all he can from you but lets you know that up front. And there's the very dangerous buyer who doesn't tell you that she is going to "steal all your chips" and does. Identify that one quickly, get out fast, and move on to your next deal. This should be another lesson to every-one, about ethics. How many people found out (through the three other parties involved) about that company's actions? I checked and discovered that the company is no longer in business. Could a lack of ethics have contributed to its disappearance? Value your reputation as an individual and an organization; you'll see how criti-cal that is to your long-term success.

P.S. Mr. Ringer, who also authored *Winning Through Intimida-tion*, has since repented of his selfish approach to selling, and spends less time looking out for number one and more time nurturing his prospects.

If I Can Get Rid of My Best Customers, I Can Salvage This Company

BANKRUPT

Tad shares his last-ditch attempt to avoid bankruptcy for his manufacturing firm

UPON FINDING MY COMPANY in financial trouble, I began a program of cutting costs and raising prices. I also needed to raise a half-million dollars in capital quickly or we were out of business. I phoned one of my largest customers.

"You need to prepay a hundred and fifty thousand dollars on your most recent order (the payment was two weeks past due)."

The general manager laughed at my absurd request and started asking about when the product would be delivered.

To make my point, I hung up on him. He called back and said he had been disconnected. I asked him if he would prefer the bank to wire the hundred and fifty thousand or overnight mail it.

He continued to complain about my late delivery and I once again hung up on him. On his next call he reminded me that he was one

134

of my largest clients, and I promptly reminded him I needed the hundred and fifty thousand and added that I was raising his price 15 percent, and I hung up again. I knew that he had to get this order from us — it would take months to shop somewhere else now — and he could lose his job.

Fifteen minutes later, he called back and asked, "What's your Federal Express number?" I lied and said we didn't have one anymore (we're cutting costs, remember?). He sent the prepayment overnight. Three months later — after all the orders were filled — he moved his account to a competitor.

I had to do this to three other customers! I burned all of these relationships because it was my quickest way out of trouble. I learned that there are always other prospects out there. But I also learned a thing or two about managing my money so I could keep those new customers as long as possible.

POSTMORTEM

THIS IS A VERY UNUSUAL and, actually, creative way to solve a problem. However, Tad might have saved a couple of the four clients by being totally honest about his situation. He might have pitched the request for money by opening with, "Buyer, are you satisfied with the parts we've built for you over the last couple of years?" Then he would explain the trouble and ask for suggestions to solve the problem. If needed, the tough-guy act could be his final fallback position. Of course, the best lesson here is, get good financial advice and don't get stuck in a hole in the first place.

Language Problems
in the Trenches

James shows how a simple phrase
— with different meanings to seller
and prospect — can wreck a big sale

OUR INVESTIGATIVE (DETECTIVE) AGENCY specializes in undercover and surveillance work. We're very good at catching worker's compensation fraud — like the guy who's taking off work and getting settlement money is same guy we've got on video roofing his house. We also have "planted" employees working in large companies. These people observe and learn which employees might be selling drugs, or stealing, or engaging in other criminal behavior.

I had secured the salesman's dream appointment: my partner and I were sitting down with one of the largest computer parts manufacturing companies in the world. And we were meeting the number-two and -three guys in the whole organization. This business was easily worth several million dollars a year to our agency.

The phrase of death for us was "domestic work." The meeting was going well until the number-two man asked, "Do you just do domestic work?" He was referring to using undercover operatives within plants in the United States. We, however, use the term "domestic work" to refer to spying on cheating husbands and digging up dirt in messy divorce cases.

"Oh, no." My partner replies. "We don't really consider that *worth our while.*"

Dead silence.

The corporate guys just stared at us in disbelief. Imagine how arrogant they thought we were. We were telling this huge player that their needs were beneath us.

At first we didn't understand the silence. By the time everyone figured out the simple misunderstanding, and explanations had been offered, the damage was done. The whole complexion of the meeting had changed. We didn't get a follow-up call from them for a long, long time. And the big contract never materialized.

I learned that you must speak a common language and not get trapped by the terminology of your industry.

 POSTMORTEM

JAMES REALIZED one of his problems: the use of industry language that confuses potential clients. He needs to realize that answering direct questions can be dangerous, too. The problem would have never occurred if he had replied, "Why do you ask that?" The prospect would have probably rephrased the question and made their understanding of the phrase clear. It was a very expensive lesson. Don't answer direct questions; ask the reason for those questions. You'll keep the prospect talking and learn more about the problems you intend to solve for them.

Five Stages of Sales Grief — A Bizarre Parallel

Thoughts on the anguish of selling malpractice

DR. ELISABETH KUBLER-ROSS has counseled thousands of patients and their families in her work on death and dying. People coping with a terminal diagnosis exhibit the classic pattern of the Five Stages of Grief:

Denial: Upon hearing the diagnosis, the patient reacts with a shocked, "No, not me!"

Anger: "Why me?" is the question that follows. Often, *blame*, directed against the doctor, nurses, and God, is a part of this stage.

Bargaining: "Yes me, but ..." "If you'll just give me five years, God, I'll ..."

Depression: Now the person is able to say, "Yes, me" with the courage to admit that it's happening, but this acknowledgment brings on depression.

Acceptance: Finally, comes acceptance, a time of facing the death calmly. This is often a difficult time for the family, since the patient tends to become withdrawn and silent.

Finally comes acceptance, *a time of facing the death of a sale calmly. This is often a difficult time since the salesperson tends to withdraw, to be silent.*

To understand that these stages are normal is to be free from the shock that occurs when they strike. We needn't fear that a person is losing his or her faith because of anger or depression; they're natural responses to this tough life situation.

For the first time in print, a bizarre parallel:

The Five Stages of Sales Grief

This is the classic pattern exhibited by salespeople coping with a terminal prospect diagnosis:

Denial: "That VP *loved* my presentation! I can't believe she's hiding behind voicemail. Our solution is perfect for her."

Anger: "Why won't she buy from me?" *Blame,* directed against the prospect, gatekeeper, and God, is often a part of this stage.

Bargaining: "I'm leaving a message that if she buys by month's end, she can have a 15 percent discount." The salesperson often believes (falsely) that lowering the price is an effective negotiating tactic.

Depression: Now the salesperson can say, "Yes, me" with the courage to admit that this prospect is not going to buy. Sadness seeps in.

Acceptance: Finally, comes acceptance, a time of facing the death of a sale calmly. This is often a difficult time, since the salesperson tends to become withdrawn and silent. "I hate selling. These things happen all the time."

To understand that these stages are normal in selling is to be free — free from the shock that occurs when this scene is repeated again and again. We needn't fear that a person is losing faith in his or her selling abilities because of anger or depression.

At some point, you'll begin to notice that you're reacting as if you're in one of these five stages. The sooner you abandon that lost sale and move on to the next one, the healthier, longer, and more rewarding your sales life will be.

Hit and Run and Basketball

Brian relates how his client/friend cost his insurance firm big bucks

TWICE A WEEK I get up at 4:30 A.M. to play basketball. For the past six years I'd gotten a great workout and plenty of clients. Wayne was one of those guys I'd played with for years. I finally landed his auto and home policies.

His coverage began on Friday, and on Sunday his car was totaled. The other guy hit him from behind, then got out of his car and ran down the street, disappearing before the police arrived.

Investigators went to an address that was no good. No one had ever heard of this person. His car had been purchased from one of those used car lots that disappear as quickly as they spring up. It was no surprise that the guilty party had no good insurance, either. So we took the hit on Wayne's total car loss.

Exactly one year and one week later, his new car was totaled! What a killer situation: my friend was going to have to fight with our claims people on the value of replacing his car, his rates would increase, and I was facing some bad blood on the basketball court. It was an embarrassing predicament.

What did I learn? I found out how to have tough conversations with people I care about.

POSTMORTEM

BRIAN GOT THE DOUBLE WHAMMY: he could lose a client and a friend. Agents normally build the foundation of their business on friends and family, so it's tricky when claims create uncomfortable situations in personal relationships. I suggest pre-selling important individual contacts with questions like, "If you have a problem with my company, how would that affect our relationship?" At least you air out potential personal problems early. On the other hand, you might decide that keeping the friendship is worth more than making the sale in the first place.

Would You Marry One?

An auto salesman reveals a verbal face-slapping wake-up call

I WAS WORKING THE COUPLE pretty hard to sell them a car. The harder they fought me with objections, the tougher — and better — I got at handling them. I felt like I was a pretty good salesman, so I took nothing personally as they did everything short of running me over during a test drive.

And then it dawned on me: I turned to the husband and said, "Oh, I get it. You know what's going on because you're in the car business!"

His wife immediately spat back in disgust, "My God! Do you think I'd have married him if he were?"

Ouch! I felt my face flush red with anger and embarrassment. I spun away from them and began to walk away. But I stopped, thinking that I'd rather take their money later and would live with their insults for now.

Of course, they didn't buy anyway.

POSTMORTEM

I LOVE THIS STORY. Not because the world needs to be any meaner to car salespeople, but because there's a little hidden mistake in the sales rep's language that caused this uncomfortable exchange of words. He made an assumption about the buyer, and it came back and bit him in the wallet. Because he assumed, then declared, that the buyer was in the car business, he actually did three things wrong. First, he insulted the wife. It doesn't matter whether her perception

141

of car sales reps is right or wrong, he still insulted her. Second, he made an inaccurate statement. The problem with this is that once you say something false, the buyer(s), consciously or otherwise, begin to mistrust you. Finally, he simply assumed something (buyer in car business) without proof.

Salespeople make these flawed assumptions frequently. It's extremely damaging to a blossoming seller/buyer relationship to make a comment that's wrong. Here's a fix for this common sales trouble: If you want to make a comment or a judgment, simply state your feelings as a *negative* question. "You're not in the car business, are you?" might have generated the same response from the prospect, but it would have left the sales rep with some dignity, since his response to the negative outburst could be, "Oh, I didn't think so." Now he has made an accurate statement, which leaves everyone on even ground, as both parties' comments are true.

A negative question is safer and won't leave you feeling stupid for having made a verbal blunder. On the other hand, if the response had been, "Yes, he *is* in the business," the rep could have made some bonding comments, like, "I knew it! Where do you work? How long have you been with that firm?" And so on. Practice rephrasing your typical sales questions in a negative format and see how much more progress you make — more often toward the close of your sales.

Firing Henry

A sales manager bemoans that breaking up is hard to do

I HATED THIS PART OF THE JOB: I had to fire Henry, one of our phone sales guys. Our telemarketing operation was staffed from local retirement homes. We had chosen Henry over the guy with the purplish-brown spray coloring his bald spot. And now Henry had to go. I asked him into my office and told him that today was his last day.

He wailed, "Oh, my God. What will my wife say? Oh, my God. Oh, no. God, no."

It was horrible. He kept wailing in an unearthly fashion for almost two minutes. I found out later that the other tele-marketers outside my office were very disturbed by the strange sounds coming from within.

I learned never to fire people until my staff has left for the day.

POSTMORTEM

THE NUMBER-ONE PROBLEM sales managers have: they don't fire unproductive reps soon enough. If you're a manager and wait too long, you mislead the poor performer ("I must be doing okay if I'm still here") and hurt the others' morale ("How bad can you be and still keep a job here? Why is that guy still here?"). Set your criteria for success and stick to those guidelines when managing your people. And if you're that sales rep who's just barely at average, don't be surprised when the ax falls. Your options are, get help or get out. How do you fire people? How have you been fired? Please remember that treating people with dignity and respect is extremely important during these uncomfortable times.

Unexpectedly Ugly Up-selling Event

Jim describes a sale gone to the dogs

I TOOK A YOUNG WOMAN AGENT, new to the insurance business, out on a call. Seventeen years' experience in selling life insurance and investment products has developed me into a resource for my manager. This means that occasionally I'm asked to take a rookie out to observe me at work in front of my clients.

143

This call was to up-sell a business owner to bigger things. I'd had a little business from him, but was now going to attempt to take over his 401(k) plan investments.

I cautioned my prot g that this was a good, solid guy with a good, solid business, *but* his office would be a mess, and that he had cats and a dog running around in the squalor.

When we arrived, the client moved several piles of papers off the two chairs in front of his desk, and we sat down and began discussing how I could enhance the performance of his stock plan.

As I moved toward a close, a strange smell began to hover in the room. At first, I thought that my rookie friend had passed gas, or that perhaps my client had. Then I realized that his Doberman had done what doggies do — left a big steaming pile right between the chairs we occupied in front of the client's desk.

Everyone was horribly embarrassed, and we quickly left without closing the deal. The tough part was that I might still have closed the guy — doggie doo and all — if my partner hadn't started gagging.

He didn't return my calls for a year.

I really believe that what happened would have been shrugged off had it been just the client and me in the office. Sadly, his embarrassment in front of the young woman was too much for him to face me again.

🏃 POSTMORTEM

WELL, THAT STINKS! One of the biggest differences between experienced and rookie sales professionals is the ability to handle the unexpected. Jim knew that he could still stay on track to up-sell this client. However, his rookie ride-along couldn't keep from physically reacting to an awful, awkward situation. Here are two suggestions for handling embarrassing scenes: First, Jim could have begun to clean up the mess (or offered to). If he had, how could the client have refused to work with him?! Secondly, Jim could have made a joke about the situation, downplaying it as a minor disruption, then returned to the conversation. Don't be afraid of taking some risk when you sell. Often, sales professionals with more guts will prevail. Don't let an awkward occurrence drain the life out of your sales call. Address it, then move on. To handle the unexpected, simply stay completely focused on your goal for that meeting.

Disappearing Client, Hiding or Dead?

Brandy recounts how a client crashed far from home

WHEN I LANDED the life policy on a hotshot entrepreneur, it was a huge boost to my selling career. The five-million-dollar policy was great for my bank account. It was even better for my credibility in the office. In an industry where women are selling in much smaller numbers than men, it was nice to see my reputation on the rise.

Shortly after he passed his medical exams and was approved, the entrepreneur began to struggle with his business. While on an unexplained trip to Eastern Europe, he was killed in a bizarre plane accident. While walking across a runway, he was sucked into an engine of the jet he was about to board.

Our firm was concerned about verifying the death in order to pay on the claim. Unlike the United States, many countries don't issue death certificates, so we hired investigators who flew across the world to interview "witnesses" to the awful scene. Some of their stories didn't quite match.

The final fishy clue proved the whole incident was a fraud perpetrated by the near-bankrupt businessman. The blood on the plane's engine belonged to a cow.

That guy still hasn't arrived back in the U.S. I guess prison is much worse than bankruptcy. And my growing reputation has been temporarily arrested, while I listen to mumbled "moos" behind my back at the office.

THIS IS A TERRIBLE STORY. How can you turn it into a positive experience? Well, the guerrilla marketer in me got really fired up when I heard it. Brandy could jump-start a promotional campaign for her business by speaking to companies and clubs around her working market territory. If her company would allow her to share this tale (some details must be left out), what group wouldn't love to hear a speaker with such a fascinating story? For Brandy herself, it's a lesson in how unpredictable life can be. The sooner we learn to just shake our heads and move on, the healthier our heads are for selling.

Saleswoman Travels into Twilight Zone

Laurie laments she can't sell anyone in town

I WAS TO GIVE A HEALTH-AND-NUTRITION lecture in a small town in New Mexico. My husband and I flew, then drove to the area, so I had no idea where we were. There weren't any gas stations to get help, no open stores, nothing. It was getting late in the afternoon, within a couple of hours of the lecture, and we were getting nervous.

I noticed a tiny town coming up and, to my surprise, I saw a banner announcing that I was to speak at the local church. Unfortunately, there were no directions, so I told my husband to pull over to a singlewide trailer with a small picket fence. It seemed to be the only place with any activity around it. I jumped out, opened the gate, and started walking across the small front yard.

As I was doing this, I began politely calling out — so no one would feel inspired to pull a gun on a stranger. I stumbled upon some higher ground, and at that moment a few people came out the door. They stopped dead in their tracks, so I stopped walking too.

The first thing I noticed was a very nasty smell. But I was more concerned about making myself appear friendly and non-threatening. All I wanted was directions to the church, I said, and mentioned that I was the speaker for the evening. The people said nothing, just looked at me in horror. For what reason, I hadn't a clue. It wasn't like I was dressed oddly, or something!

Again I asked if they could direct me to the church, in case they'd failed to hear me the first time. A man walked up to me and quietly asked, "Could you please step back three feet?"

"Sure," I said, and moved onto lower ground.

It seems I'd been standing on his newly deceased wife's very fresh grave.

Then, he ever so politely gave me directions, but I was so shocked by my failure to see that I'd been standing on a grave (and sinking into the dirt, mind you), that I only got the general direction he was pointing.

Needless to say, the church was quite surprised at how few people showed up for this lecture. They'd been promoting it for weeks, had put up banners and more.

I remember exactly what the wife of the clergyman said: "It's not like there's anything to do around here but die. We don't even get good TV!"

POSTMORTEM

LAURIE ANALYZES WHAT HAPPENED: "Bet you can guess how many sales I made that evening — zero. I'm very sure this man began calling everyone he knew to tell them of my insensitivity, and encourage them not to go to the lecture. It was a *very* expensive lesson, and to this day a horribly embarrassing memory. Be very conscious of where you walk — it could be on the grave of your next sale." Laurie learned a lesson about sales call preparation. At the risk of stating the obvious, do your homework if you travel, and map out your calls so you aren't late. It's the professional approach to handling a territory.

147

Shooting Suspects

How to make a successful sale through the power of psychological triggers.

Joe Sugarman, BluBlocker sunglasses millionaire, offers insights on how two psychological triggers can quickly establish expertise with prospects.

A DESIRE TO BUY SOMETHING often involves a subconscious decision. In fact, I claim that 95 percent of buying decisions are indeed subconscious. Knowing the subconscious reasons why people buy, and using this information in a fair and constructive way, will trigger greater sales response — often far beyond what you could imagine.

In my book, *Triggers*, I talk about the critical effect of credibility and the strength of specificity in positioning an individual or company as an expert resource for potential customers. Here are some key strategies you can implement that utilize credibility and specificity.

Credibility is a reflection of the quality of a service or product that you offer. It is revealed in seven ways:

1. Magazines or newspapers in which I advertise. If I advertise my product in the *Wall Street Journal*, I'm piggybacking onto their credibility and their constant vigilance against their readers being taken advantage of. On the other hand, if I placed that same ad in the *National Enquirer*, I take on the credibility — or lack thereof — that this publication has established with readers. Again, the environment in which you are selling affects your credibility.

2. You can also enhance credibility through the use of a brand-name product. For example, if I'm offering an electronic product by the name of Yorx, with the exact same features as one whose

brand name is Sony, which one has more credibility? The Sony would probably sell better — even if its price were higher.

3. Adding an appropriate celebrity endorser is another effective way to enhance credibility.

4. The name of a company can affect its credibility too. A company called The Tool Shack sold computers. This name actually detracted from the credibility of the product they were selling.

5. Sometimes a city or state can add credibility. That's why some companies locate in larger cities. If I were in publishing, I would want my offices in New York City, the "Publishing Capital of the World."

6. If I had to have brain surgery, I'd want a top surgeon with impressive credentials, not someone who walks in with a book entitled, *Brain Surgery for Dummies*. The credentials and the top people are both important in establishing credibility.

7. One technique I used in my mail order ads to build credibility was inserting a technical explanation to add a certain expertise to my message. A good example of this technique is the following caption, which I wrote for a picture of the integrated circuit in a watch:

A pin points to the new decoder/driver integrated circuit, which takes the input from the oscillator countdown integrated circuit and computes the time while driving the display. This single space-age device replaces thousands of solid-state circuits and provides the utmost reliability — all unique to Sensor.

Very few people would be able to understand this technical commentary. In fact, when I sent the ad to the manufacturer for approval, he called my attention to the caption under the picture and said, "What you wrote there is correct, but who's going to understand it? Why did you even use it?"

Providing a technical explanation that the reader might not understand shows that we really did our research: if we say it's good, knowing what we know, then it must be good. It gives the buyer confidence that he or she is indeed dealing with an expert. Incidentally, the watch was one of our best-selling products.

In a mail-order ad or in person, technical explanations can add a great deal of credibility, but you must make sure that you indeed become an expert, and your statements must be accurate. If not, the buyer will see right through the ploy.

There are many ways to add credibility, and realizing this is important when you're crafting your sales presentation and creating the selling environment for your product. Use the methods explained here as a checklist to determine which techniques make sense for what you're selling and then use them discreetly. They are indeed very powerful when included in a well-crafted sales presentation.

In my BluBlocker Sunglasses infomercials, I state the specific reasons why blue light isn't good for your eyes.

Specificity refers to the power of detailed and precise statements to support your credibility.

Let me give you an example: If I say, "New dentists everywhere use and recommend CapSnap Toothpaste," it sounds like typical advertising lingo — puffery designed to sell a product. It's so general that it will probably cause a prospect to discount the statement you've just made and maybe everything else you say. But if I say, "Ninety-two percent of new dentists use and recommend CapSnap Toothpaste," it sounds much more believable. The consumer is likely to think that we did a scientific survey and that 92 percent of the dentists actually use the toothpaste.

When people perceive certain general statements as puffery or typical advertising babble, those statements are at best discounted or accepted with some doubts. In contrast, statements with specific facts can generate strong believability. Of course, the specific facts must be honest and accurate.

In my BluBlocker Sunglasses infomercials, I state the specific reasons why blue light isn't good for your eyes. I explain that blue light focuses in front of the retina (which is the focusing screen of the eye) and not on the retina as do other colors. So when you block blue light, you block those rays that don't focus on your retina, and therefore objects appear clearer, sharper, and more defined. I'm specific. It sounds believable. And the statement is a lot better than just saying, "BluBlocker sunglasses let you see clearer, sharper, and with more definition."

If you're describing a product that works with the circulatory functions of the body, you can talk about "242 miles of blood vessels," instead of "miles of blood vessels." When you talk about feet, instead of saying, "There are a lot of nerve endings in the bottoms of your feet '" you can say instead, "There are seventy-two thousand nerve endings at the bottoms of your feet." You're stating a fact and being specific, as opposed to making a general or vague statement. You are more believable. You have more credibility.

There's one other benefit to being specific: By being specific you sound like you're an expert on your product; you imply that you've really investigated it and are very knowledgeable. This too builds trust and confidence.

People are generally very skeptical about advertising, and often don't believe many of the claims stated in ads. But when you make a specific claim using precise facts and figures, your message is much more credible and is often trusted.

Be specific in your statements and your facts to build credibility and believability. The use of these triggers in your communications can make you considerably more successful than your competition — and dramatically boost your income. Learn them now and start using them tomorrow. And then watch your sales soar.

JOE SUGARMAN is the author of one of the most valuable sales and marketing books you can own, *Triggers: 30 Ways to Control the Mind of Your Prospect to Motivate, Influence and Persuade.* Go buy this book today! Joe is also the world-famous entrepreneur who sold twenty million pairs of BluBlocker sunglasses.

Resurrection

Part Six

Resurrection —
Life After the Death
of 20ᵗʰ Century Selling

Is THERE HOPE for the millions of sales professionals out there? Yes. At www.SalesAutopsy.com, we do believe in resurrection. To speed up your journey back from the selling dead, read the three sections below that offer solutions to our four characters, the key tool you need to get great at the wisdom of selling, and twenty ways that training will help you take home more money.

Solutions for the
Sales Scoundrels

Fixing Our Four Characters

Put the Sales Dinosaur in a Museum

You can identify the Dinosaur by noticing a rep who talks too much, uses outdated sales techniques, and attempts to manipulate prospects.

Have you learned to sell from books and tapes published in the 1980s? Hasn't life changed significantly since then? We've gone from typewriters to word processors, to personal computers, to wireless communication devices. Many of us are selling products and services that didn't even exist when some of these sales books were written! Everyone has been exposed to these old techniques for twenty to thirty years.

It's time to utilize selling approaches that are new to buyers *and* that distinguish us from ordinary salespeople. Here are your three moves toward freedom from dull, uninspired selling:

1. Recognize that old often equals overused and possibly useless.
2. Begin upgrading your sales techniques now.
3. Start with one unique new selling approach.

If you steal a banana, later steal a book,
then later steal a Buick – you'll awaken
one morning surrounded by steel bars
and a new set of friends.

In our stories, we've seen the effects of old techniques, so let's get to the upgrade right now. *Upgrade* is a great word, because we all know that our computerized world is always improving, and upgrades are the standard method for us to acquire more effective and efficient practices. You new strategy is to focus your discussions with prospects on one thing — *consequences*. These are the consequences of the prospect's current problem or future problem. These problems occur because your prospect is not using your solution.

How Consequences Work So Well

The number-one rule in raising children is to teach them that an outcome or aftereffect occurs as a result of their actions. These repercussions can be good or bad, but let's focus on the bad fallout of their actions. If you touch the hot stove, you burn your hand. Let's move forward a few years. If you steal a banana, later steal a book, then later steal a Buick, you'll awaken one morning surrounded by steel bars and a new set of friends.

Consequences reveal that the initial problem, don't touch the hot stove, is not the real problem. The real problems are the many repercussions of touching the hot stove: you burn your hand, so you can't play baseball today, so you lose your starting position, so you can't make the all-star team, and so on. We want to learn to travel as far down that path as we can get the prospect to walk with us.

In our sales lives, we want to talk about how the repercussions of not buying from us could damage the prospect's business in some way. Consequences might include a slow-down in sales, diminished production, angry shareholders, serious damage to the future of the business, etc. Your job is to point the prospect to the real aftermath of his or her unsolved trouble. Let's look at a quick example of how this might occur on a call:

You: You asked to meet me because of what concern?

Prospect: We need a gift to give our sales force at the national convention. And we want to get the right type of gift this year.

You: So what happens if you don't get the right kind of gift?

Prospect: Well, last year we bought this fun, frivolous electronic device. It was cute and unique, but didn't have a lasting impact or inspire the team to perform better.

You: So they didn't perform better?

Prospect: Exactly. Our next quarter's sales were flat — actually the same as prior to the conference. That's not good.

You: It's not good because … (prompting for consequences)?

Prospect: I got blamed for wasting fifty thousand dollars on a dumb gift for five thousand sales reps. At times I was made to feel like I was responsible for the next quarter's mediocre performance.

You: Well, you've been here a long time; people probably really respect you regardless.

Prospect: But right now, some don't and I'm not happy about it. All because I thought I chose a cool gift for our sales team.

You: I'm sorry that experience was so tough on you. So, if you chose something that both educated and entertained your salespeople, would that make more sense?

Prospect: What do you have in mind?

And we're off to the races, finish line in sight!

Did you see how the consequences of wasted money and blame for bad decision making were brought into play by good questioning that directed the conversation toward the impact of the wrong decision?

Did you notice how the *personal* consequences to the prospect (his reputation was at risk) create more motivation toward change than just *company* consequences (wasted money)? Dig deep for the personal impact of the problem your prospect describes.

A tourist is much like a seagull. It goes about dumping on everyone and everything. Then soaring away upon any wind that blows, it leaves a mess behind.

Take that dinosaur and bury his bones deep. Choose to teach your prospects about consequences today.

For a detailed description on how you can use this strategy to script high impact conversations with your potential clients, see the mini-workshop in the appendix.

Send the Sales Tourist Home

You can identify the Tourist by seeing someone new to selling, poorly trained, or not taking his or her selling career seriously.

A tourist is much like a seagull. It goes about dumping on everyone and everything. Then, soaring away upon any wind that blows, it leaves a mess behind.

You might not be a Tourist by intention. You might be new to the sales profession. You might be experienced, but frustrated because you have lots of activity and little money to show for it. Whatever your situation, you're not acting as sharp and skilled as you could be. Don't despair. Before you decide to head home and find a "real job," take some of these thoughts to heart. Here's your first move to becoming a sales professional:

Act professionally from the minute you begin thinking about work today. Remember that God is not the only person watching you. The payoff in becoming a sales professional is like no other job you can find (unless you have the talent to become a professional athlete, and that's a one-in-a-million shot). I remember recruiting a medical sales rep who took a job and got to choose his compensation package. He could elect to be paid a base salary of sixty thousand plus commissions, or no salary and a much higher commission percentage. This guy was a real pro, so what did he choose? It was straight commission — without a moment's hesitation. He told me that he could make either a hundred and fifty thousand or three hundred thousand dollars. His behavior was so highly skilled and regimented that he had no fear about working for no base salary. He knew he was going to take home three hundred thousand in the coming year. That's a nice payoff for paying your dues in the selling world.

Travel back from Tourist mode with the strategy that world-class sales professionals employ. You want to develop the disciplined behavior these extraordinary earners practice every day to make great money. Regardless of what level of experience you've achieved in your sales career, implement these three steps immediately:

1. Define and write down what goal you want to acquire.
2. Set a time frame for acquiring your goal.
3. Pretend you've already gotten your hands on that goal, then *work backward* to determine what activities it would take to attain it.

Here's a simple example of how to work backward to identify your success path to your goal:

Your goal is to pay cash for a new Infiniti automobile, which costs sixty thousand dollars. You want to be driving it within one year. Follow these steps to create a professional plan for your daily work activities:

- You make a five-hundred-dollar commission for each sale.
- You need a hundred and twenty sales to award yourself the car.
- This means you need ten sales each month.
- You close 20 percent of your face-to-face sales calls.
- So you need to get in front of fifty buyers a month to close those ten.
- You have twenty-five workdays each month, so you need two sales calls per day.
- If you get appointments with one of four phone contacts, you need to contact two hundred people to get your fifty appointments.

- Two hundred divided by twenty-five days = eight daily phone contacts.

- You need eight phone calls and two meetings each day to earn your sixty-thousand-dollar car.

All this activity drives your regular behavior on the job. By employing these guidelines you develop a professional attack on your marketplace.

Work through these steps with your own figures to determine your daily activity. You'll be perceived as a pro. You'll feel like a pro. You'll pay yourself like a pro.

Banish the Sales Napoleon to an Island

You can identify the Napoleon by noticing a bad attitude and a big ego with occasional splashes of anger.

When Napoleon was finally defeated, he was sent to live the rest of his life on the island of St. Helena. Here, in isolation, the emperor and his ego could do no more damage to Europe and surrounding territories.

The ego lies at the root of this character. The best performers use their egos to motivate themselves. They don't use egos to do damage to other relationships.

Your ability to control your ego is manifested by your attitude toward three areas of your life:

1. The company you work for — especially if it's your own.
2. The marketplace into which you sell.
3. The way you feel about *you*.

Strong, healthy feelings about all three of these areas will give you a winning attitude. If you're falling down in one of these areas, you need to change that area or your attitude about it. If you need to change companies, do it now. If you need to change the market to which you sell, go find another animal to hunt in a different place. If you need to change an unhealthy area of your life — physical, mental, or spiritual — get growing in it. Yes, that's *growing* rather than *going*.

*When you experience growing pains as you develop a
better business approach, your bank account will
experience growing pains as well.*

With a physically fit attitude about who you are and what you do
you'll be able to set your ego aside during the selling process and
choose commissions over conflict. The best performers don't stuff
their egos into the faces of co-workers and customers (and friends
and family). They are humble, because they want to accomplish
their desire to close the sale. Lose the battle and win the war for
your prospect's money. Exile that ego and you'll keep a tight rein
on a healthy attitude.

Look at it this way: When you experience growing pains as you
develop a better business approach, your bank account will experience growing pains as well.

Shoot Down the Sales Maverick

You can identify the Maverick by noticing someone who loves
to handle life on the fly. They rarely plan and won't use a selling
system.

The Sales Maverick was very successful from World War I through
the 1980s. In the First World War, there were very few instruments
on planes, so the pilots literally flew by the seat of their pants. Many
didn't even have maps to guide them to their targets or goals. They
simply learned from survivors who got there first. They had no
models for success so they learned "on the job."

This is the cause for sales performances that fluctuates as wildly
as John Travolta's acting career. No one is comfortable with
unpredictability. Wildly fluctuating earnings will frustrate any salesperson, and can also devastate his or her home life. This
unpredictability is a serious sickness that can infect an organization
with a Maverick aboard. Managers and sales colleagues are confused by a Maverick's mixed periods of great success and dramatic
failure. Use a selling system to get out of Maverick mode.

The term *system* refers to the use of a model that copies the success of others. The system tells us what to say at the beginning of
each sales call. It shows us a path to follow when encountering tough

159

prospects, handling objections, filling out paperwork, even planning the pieces of each workday — like the times we do phone calling and when we have face-to-face appointments.

Learning on the job in the sales world means practicing on prospects. You don't want to learn on the job in selling, you want to learn off the job.

If I could offer compelling words to inspire you to use a system, they would be: The ability to predict the future is one definition of an excellent manager. A system helps predict the future of each sales call. It predicts the future of each sales rep. Your accuracy in assessing what will happen next is a large part of your comfort and satisfaction with your job. For example, think of all the times you've left a prospect with the belief that "We'll talk again soon," only to find him or her hiding behind voicemail when you thought it was a good sales call with good potential for a sale. The frustration of doubt and its partner, lack of confidence, can discourage the best sales rep and manager. Don't let the Maverick in you mangle your confidence. Put a system in place to insure predictability. Some benefits of using a selling system are:

1. It duplicates successful behavior
2. It disqualifies bad prospects quickly
3. It employs strategies that allow you, not the prospect, to control the sales process

The other key piece of using a system is the ability to practice.

Could you play in the NBA? Or the WNBA? Professional athletes practice during the season and the off-season. What do they practice? They work their skills and their system to hone every fine detail to perfection. Would you like to be an NBA-level sales professional?

Trained salespeople continually practice in class and inside their company at sales meetings. Salespeople who get their only learning from books and tapes tend to practice techniques at random *on their prospects*. This type of learner can never really "own" techniques and strategies until he or she has used them many, many times. The

160

strategies and language needed to achieve NBA-level selling skills will take so long to achieve in this manner that one can become frustrated, even disgusted, about one's selling career. Learning on the job in the sales world means practicing on prospects. You don't want to learn on the job in selling; you want to learn off the job.

Your best move to achieve significant success in selling is to get yourself into an ongoing class. This is not just a one-day seminar or weekend event. It's a class that meets weekly for six months, a year, or longer. It's a class that teaches you how to sell while letting you practice what you're learning. It's a class offering true training that becomes a part of you. This graduate-level education lasts a lifetime, and pays you back in huge dividends: much higher earnings.

If I can get you to take away one bit of wisdom from this book, let it be this:

Find A Selling System, Learn It, and Use It.

Have A Bagel

Five Bites to Bigger Sales Success

World-class behavioral skills and NLP trainer Robert Dilts developed the B.A.G.E.L. Model for teaching sales professionals how to notice and use the "hidden" clues that prospects offer about their decision-making strategies.

YOUR PROSPECTS EXPRESS THEIR MENTAL PROCESSES with the help of certain physiological hints. You can learn to observe these five physical reactions to gather rich data that will help you experience rapport and close more sales.

The primary behavioral elements you want to note are:

Body Postures

Accessing Cues

Gestures

Eye movements

Language Patterns

1. Body Posture

People often assume systematic, habitual postures when deep in thought. Some typical examples:

A prospect who tends to be *visual* leans back, with head and shoulders up, and exhibits shallow breathing.

A prospect who tends to be *auditory* leans forward, head cocked to the side, shoulders back, and arms folded.

A prospect who tends to be *kinesthetic* has head and shoulders down and exhibits deep breathing.

2. Accessing Cues

When people are thinking, they reveal their thinking processes in a number of different ways, including: breathing rate, nonverbal grunts and groans, facial expressions, snapping their fingers, scratching their heads, and so on. For example:

A *visual* prospect reveals high shallow breathing, squinting eyes, a higher-pitched voice, and a faster tempo.

An *auditory* prospect reveals full breathing from the chest, a knitted brow, and a fluctuating voice tone and tempo.

A *kinesthetic* prospect reveals deep breathing from the lower belly, and a deep breathy voice with a slower tempo.

Visual   Auditory   Kinesthetic

3. Gestures

People will often touch, point to, or use gestures indicating the sense organ they're using to think. Some typical examples:

Visual prospects touch or point to the eyes; their gestures are made above eye level.

Auditory prospects point toward or gesture near the ears; they touch the mouth or jaw.

Kinesthetic prospects touch the chest and stomach; their gestures are made below the neck.

4. Eye Movements

Automatic, unconscious eye movements often accompany particular thought processes, indicating the use of visual, auditory, or kinesthetic thinking. We've categorized these cues into the following pattern:

Eye Movement Patterns

5. Language Patterns

Prospects often use words that reflect their thinking processes. Verbs, adverbs, and adjectives are typically selected at an unconscious level, and so offer clues to the prospect's information-processing patterns. For example:

Visual: I *see* what you are saying. That doesn't look quite right. I need to get clear on this idea. The concept is sort of hazy to me right now. I just go blank. That casts some light on the subject. We need a new perspective. That is a colorful example.

Auditory: That rings a bell. I hear you. It sounds good to me. Listen to this. Everything just suddenly clicked. Tune in to what they're trying to say. I had to ask myself. That idea has been rattling around in my head for a while.

Kinesthetic: I've got a good feeling about this project. I need to get a handle on this. He needs to get in touch with the flow of the sentiment. You have a solid proposal. We're up against a wall. That's a heavy problem. Can you grasp what needs to be done? A list of common sensory-based words:

VISUAL	AUDITORY	KINESTHETIC
see	*hear*	*grasp*
look	*listen*	*touch*
sight	*sound*	*feeling*
clear	*resonant*	*solid*
bright	*loud*	*heavy*
picture	*word*	*handle*
hazy	*noisy*	*rough*
brings to light	*rings a bell*	*connects*
show	*tell*	*move*

Your ability to pick up as many of these "hidden" clues as possible will affect how well you gain rapport with prospects. Simply communicate in a matching fashion, visual words for a visually oriented prospect, and so on. This use of a "dialect" that works best for each prospect will significantly increase the quality of your conversations. It increases your ability to communicate your sales message so that it makes the most "sensory" sense to your prospect. Remember that people prefer to deal with those who are like them. It will amaze you how a taste of your B.A.G.E.L. when you're talking to prospects (and family and friends) helps you get to know people and turn them into clients.

Robert Dilts has had a global reputation as a leading behavioral skills trainer and business consultant since the 1970s. He is an expert on success modeling and it's application to leadership, creativity, communication, and team development.

Robert recommends that salespeople wanting more skills in this fascinating area of understanding the brain read the book, *Applications of NLP*, from Meta Publications, 831-464-0254. His most recent thinking would be in the NLP Encyclopedia: www.nlpuniversitypress.com.

Robert's website is: www.nlpu.com.

Unique or Antique?
Be outstanding in your field
or you'll be **left out**
standing in your field

WHEN SPEAKING ON CREATIVITY and the value of mental flexibility for salespeople, I often open with this question: What do you think of when the word *holiday* is mentioned? The answers fall into several categories ranging from specific, "December 25," to general, "Days off of work." They range from personal, "Eating a big meal with the family," to international, "Christmas Day." Consider this tale and how *holiday* is defined in a creative, unexpected way:

It's common knowledge that Adolf Hitler was an avid devotee of the occult. He often consulted several astrologers to determine his actions. He even looked to them for advice about engaging the enemy in battle.

One day, the F hrer called his chief astrologer and said, "Is it possible to discover the day on which I will die?"

"Oh," said the man, "I know the day you will die."

Startled, Hitler demanded he continue.

"You will die on a Jewish holiday," the astrologer said.

"Which Jewish holiday will I die on?" asked Hitler.

"Well," concluded the man, "*any day you die will be a Jewish holiday.*"

What occurs in this joke is a perfect example of mental flexibility — thinking out of the box, if you prefer. The definition of *holiday* can come from many directions and still be accurate and true. While the astrologer's definition is completely unforeseen, it's still true. This is what makes a joke humorous. The punch line is totally unexpected, yet perfectly logical.

Okay, you're thinking. That's entertaining, but what's the big deal about this concept? How does it make a difference in the life of a sales professional? Let's look at what a very large selling organization is learning about the value of creativity.

At a national sales conference for Coca-Cola, Jeffrey Gitomer, speaker, syndicated writer, and author of *The Sales Bible,* paces the stage and wrings his hands in frustration. "Here's the problem," he says. "If you cannot distinguish yourself from the competition, you will only sell based on price."

Jeffrey stops abruptly and points at the crowd. "How do you distinguish yourself? It's not with your voicemail like this, is it? 'Hello, I'm on the phone or out of the office ...' Well, duh!" The laughter that follows reinforces the point. Ordinary is pretty scary. It can cost you money in lost sales.

And while low pricing is a legitimate business strategy, only one company can sit on the bottom rung of the pricing ladder. And if you're positioned higher up, you have a problem — you need a different selling strategy.

How would you answer Jeffrey Gitomer's question? If you're not memorable as a company and an individual, your message will be lost in the noise of the thousands of daily sales messages blathering for your prospects' attention.

The answer is, you distinguish yourself by presenting yourself as a rare bird in the eyes of your prospect. You need to be unique and therefore memorable.

To do this you'll need to employ creative thinking in two areas of your business: You need to be positioned uniquely as a company, and you need to present yourself uniquely as an individual. Here are examples of both:

Ray Bard's unique streak positions his company as the elite organization in his industry

One of their newest books, Marketing Outrageously, *has a cover showing a sumo wrestler dunking a basketball.*

ONE OF MY FAVORITE best-selling stories is about a company in the best-selling business. Bard Press Publishing (www.bardpress.com) produced nineteen books from 1996–2001. Ten have become bestsellers. A 53 percent bestseller rate in an industry that produces sixty thousand products a year? That's an incredible accomplishment. Their unique, striking book covers get snatched off the shelves of bookstores at a rate that thousands of authors would kill for. One of their newest books, *Marketing Outrageously,* has a cover showing a sumo wrestler dunking a basketball. Their content is unique, as well, as you'll see if you pick up *The Wizard of Ads,* by one of our guest gurus, Roy H. Williams. (See page 44)

My unique streak solves two selling problems.

She wouldn't take my calls or return them. I could not get an appointment with this CFO. She managed the financial present and future of one of the largest hospitals in Chicago, and I had a great new service she would want. I almost gave up after having been ignored for two months.

Then I remembered the coconut!

I dug into my guerrilla-marketing file and found the brochure from a Hawaiian company that mailed coconuts. They wrote your message on them in black marker. I placed my order and sent it off with the words, "You're a tough nut to crack."

A week later my phone rang. I answered and heard nothing but laughter.

"I'm sitting here at my desk and my secretary and I are dying laughing," the CFO said. "When would you like to come in?"

It worked! An action that was totally unexpected, but perfectly logical had gotten me in.

I needed a similarly unique strategy when I required a fast filing of some documents for a government office with the State of Illinois.

The woman who managed that government department was a tyrant. She was blunt and wielded her power with sledgehammer-like rudeness. I was about to meet her for the first time.

I walked into the office and told her what I needed and that I needed it right away. She scowled and began to shake her head.

From behind my back I produced a plant. "I know that we've never met before, but the people you normally deal with told me that you were a hard-nosed, but hardworking dragon, and that you were awful to rub shoulders with. So I thought it would be appropriate to give you a plant that reflects your personality."

I handed her the cactus.

She laughed and couldn't stop laughing. "It's true! That's me. This is perfect."

I got my paperwork handled on the spot.

Totally unexpected, but perfectly logical. My unique streak saved my tail in both situations.

Your unique streak is your secret weapon in selling.

Stretch your brain and build your confidence that you can look at sales problems in a new light. You can discover creative ways to develop your unique streak!

 Coconuts and cacti are just two of thousands of products you can use to distinguish yourself from the ordinary salespeople out there. Where do you find inexpensive "toys" to tantalize and train your prospects into the perception that you're one of a kind?

There's a whole industry built around making unique impressions. It is the Premium Incentive Industry. American businesses spent $22.8 billion on merchandise and travel for motivational use in 1996.

For lower-priced products like hats, pens, T-shirts and more, you want to work with the Advertising Specialty Institute (ASI). Go to their website www.promomart.com to find more than 140,000 products. Products can be selected by industry. You can also find a local distributor who will come to you with creative ideas and products that will help position you as a unique sales professional or organization. These are the people who can brand your company name on coffee cups, and caps, and coconuts.

For higher-priced products, like televisions, travel gifts and more, you want to check out the Incentive Marketing Association (www.incentivemarketing.org). You can attend their national tradeshows in Chicago (www.motivationshow.com) or New York (www.piexpo.com), and just walk the aisles for creative ideas. You can receive their monthly magazines free of charge. Check out the website www.supplierfinder.com for product ideas and supplier help. The national trade association for the industry is the Incentive Marketing Association, www.incentivemarketing.org in Naperville, IL, USA 630-369-7780.

You can achieve a unique position in the mind of your prospect. Your ability to be perceived as unique and to conquer your niche is critical to avoid the mediocrity of the ordinary. Decide today that you will not be just an ordinary salesperson. Find something special to wear, to give away, and to say, and you will be remembered and paid well for it.

Lead Generation Leapfrogging

How using referral incentives can move you up and beyond the competition

Business Network International founder and best-selling author Dr. Ivan Misner reveals how recognition leads to riches

EVERYBODY LOVES REFERRALS, and one thing I've learned is that people also love to be recognized for giving referrals. Experienced business professionals agree that referrals are easier to close, have fewer complaints, are more loyal, more trusting, and remain clients longer.

Creativity is the key to any good incentive program.

A survey that Robert Davis and I conducted (published in our book, *Business By Referral*), found incentives to be one of the most important methods of generating referrals for successful business professionals. Incentives can range from simple recognition, such as a thank you, to monetary rewards based on business generated. Nearly 25 percent of all the respondents in the international survey we conducted considered incentives an effective generator of referrals.

Creativity is the key to any good incentive program. People just naturally like to help each other, but especially when they know their efforts are successful. Let your contact know when a referral he or she has made comes through, and be as creative as you can.

I've heard many novel ways that businesspeople reward those who send them referrals. A female consultant sends bouquets of flowers to men. The owner of a music store sends concert tickets. A financial planner sends change purses and money clips.

An accountant in St. Louis thanks those who successfully refer a client to him by paying for a dinner for two at an exclusive restaurant at least one hour's drive from their homes. This approach firmly plants the accountant in the minds of his referral sources: they won't be able to use it right away because the distance requires that they plan for it. Because it has been planned, they'll be talking about it as the date approaches, and probably about the accountant. Later, when the referring party runs into someone else who might need an accountant, whom will he or she recommend?

A realtor I met in northern California told me that for almost six years he had offered a hundred-dollar finder's fee to anyone giving him a referral that led to a listing or sale. He said that in all that time, he had given only about a dozen finder's fees, so he decided to try another kind of incentive.

Living on a large parcel of land in prime wine country, he had begun growing grapes in his own vineyard. A thought had occurred to him: Why not take the next step? He began processing the grapes and bottling his own special vintage wine. After the first harvest, he had a graphic artist design a beautiful label, which he affixed to each bottle. He told all his friends that he did not sell this wine; he gave it as a gift to anyone providing him with a bona fide referral.

He gave away dozens of cases in the first three years, half the time it took him to give only a dozen cash finder's fees. Yet, each bottle cost him less than ten dollars to produce. This special vintage wine makes him infinitely more money than giving away a handful of hundred-dollar bills.

About two weeks after the first edition of this book went to print I got a call from the realtor. "Has your book gone to print?" he asked. I told him it had.

Too bad," he replied. "I've got a terrific story for you."

Last Friday I got a phone call from a woman I didn't know. Out of the blue, she gave me two referrals. As I wrote down the information, I asked her how she had heard of me.

"I had dinner last night at a friend's house. He served wine. I took a sip. 'Great wine!' I told him. 'Where did you buy it?'

'You can't buy it, he said. The only way you can get it is to give this real estate agent a referral.'

"I have two referrals," she said. "Can I get two bottles?"

"So I gladly sent her two bottles. Both referrals turned into business, and each of them cost me only ten dollars."

It sometimes amazes me, even now, how something as simple as a bottle of wine can be such a powerful incentive for people to give you referrals. But the explanation is really quite simple: it's special. A bottle of wine that can't be bought can be worth ten times what it cost to produce when it's traded for something as valuable as a business referral.

Incentives for those around you

Are there employees, co-workers, friends, or relatives who might be able to refer you? It always surprises me that people forget to provide the incentives for the individuals working with them. You'll probably need to offer different kinds of incentives for different groups of people. You might choose to offer something completely different to your employees (such as bonuses and vacation days) than you would to your clients or networking associates (perhaps unique and useful gifts).

Remember: Most individuals who are preparing to score big by building word-of-mouth business consider finding the right incentive the biggest challenge. To make it easier on yourself, be sure to get feedback from others who have a significant interest in your success.

Don't underestimate the value of recognizing the people who send you business. A well-thought-out incentive program will add much to your word-of-mouth program.

Dr. Ivan Misner is founder and CEO of BNI (www.bni.com), the world's largest referral organization, with more than two thousand chapters throughout North America, Europe, Asia, Africa, and Australia. He is the author of the best-selling books, Masters of Networking, 7 Second Marketing, and the World's Best-Known Marketing Secret.

Dan's Lifetime of Lessons List

Trumpet	Accordion	Softball	Scuba
NLP	Sales	Driving	Table tennis
Speaking	Dancing	Potty training	Tying shoelaces
Real estate	Budgeting	Software	Memory training
Tennis	Taekwondo	Photo-reading	Headhunting

Look at all the training I've had in my lifetime. Yes, there are some strange ones in there. Take the time to make a list yourself. It's a fascinating reflection on what you felt was important enough, at different stages of your life, to acquire expert help to improve yourself.

How many of those lessons do you continue to use? You can skip the potty training and shoelace tying and get right to the serious stuff. Is there anything missing from your list? Since this is about sales training, is that on your list? If you've been trained to sell, are you applying the training every day?

Training the Troops: Transformation or Trouble?

THIS STORY IS A BAD ONE. You would recognize the name of the credit card organization, but I can't mention it here: people who confess their selling disasters are guaranteed anonymity.

A huge contract had been signed. Someone had sold/fooled the credit card company into believing they were going to get effective training. Reps were flown in from all over the country to go through the class. A bored "trainer" from the training organization sat at the back of the class and read verbatim from a manual while changing slides on a screen. The trainees had the difficult decision of figuring out whether to read the manual in front of them, listen to it being read, or read it on the screen. The VP of sales who shared this story was horrified when she sat in on a class. The training had virtually zero impact on the reps. The company's hopes for better performance were crushed like a bug on a windshield. They knew quickly that someone had made a bad decision when they invited that training group to "school" their sales team.

Training can create a dramatic increase in your earnings. It can also be a bad investment that wastes time and money. The following information reveals the attack plan of great training. You'll discover which places in the sales path are roadblocks to selling success. You'll also realize how you benefit by learning to leap over these blocks. The information is first laid out for the individual sales professional, and then for the entrepreneur, manager, or sales trainer.

For more detailed information on how you can identify a quality training organization, as well as some success stories from individuals and organizations being trained, pick up the white paper on training at www.SalesAutopsy.com/book.

What Makes Training So Valuable?

If you want to win the Indianapolis 500, do you buy gas at the cheapest no-name gas station in town? To win a marathon, do you eat Twinkies? The highest value of training is that it helps you close, that is, cross the line in first place, much more often. Your most important concern right now should be how to build a selling methodology into your sales life or sales organization. Here's a fascinating list of the places along the selling path where we all stumble. Fix these and you improve performance, increase peace of mind, and take more money home. Ignore them and you die a slow death on the selling battlefield.

Sales Professional, How Well Do You Feed Your Family?

Eating beans, chicken or steak tonight?

A SYSTEM MAKES YOUR LIFE EASIER because you realize the following:
1. Turn your back on failure; learn when to walk away. A system helps you qualify or disqualify prospects early in the sales process, so you don't spend time and energy on people who won't or can't spend money on you.

2. Hate spiders and snakes? There are no surprises. A system shows you, ahead of time, how to deal with each situation as it arises.

3. Prophets = profits. You can glimpse the future. A system forces you to get a commitment from the prospect. This keeps you on track by knowing and focusing on the next steps in the sales process.

4. Number-one draft picks apply here. You'll always be perceived as a pro. A system scripts your phone and face-to-face conversations, which keeps you from sounding or acting unprofessional by stumbling over words or seeming unsure of yourself.

5. Who's running this show anyway? You know who's in charge — it's you. A system keeps you in control of the sales process and doesn't allow the prospect to control you.

6. Idle hands are the devil's workshop. You'll never wonder how to utilize your time. A system simplifies your whole workday because all your activities are pre-planned. You never spend time wondering which action to engage in next. This also aids eliminating call reluctance.

7. The best things in life are ... STOP! No free coaching for prospects. A system keeps you from doing unpaid consulting.

8. Whose turn to take out the trash? Define responsibilities. You clearly spell out the roles of the buyer and seller during the process.

9. Charging credit card or charging bull. A system creates a mandatory procedure in the selling process to address the money issues. You can keep the prospect from hiding the budget and messing with your head about when and how much money will be available to solve the problem at hand. (Hint: You don't wait till the end of the call to find out if money is available)

10. Beggars can be losers. A system enforces a method to allow the rep to determine what would *really* motivate the buyer to become a client.

Of these ten points, select just two or three that you struggle with. Think about what a difference it would make if you had the map to avoid these roadblocks.

Please, sales professional, please find a selling system, learn it, and use it. If your company won't pay for training or doesn't provide adequate training, you need to make a decision: Is training an investment in your career, earnings, and family, or will you eat beans tonight?

Entrepreneur, Sales Manager or Trainer: How Well Do You Manage and Motivate?

Do your salespeople smell like beans, chicken or steak?

IMPLEMENTING A SALES METHOD might be the missing link to the future of your firm. Do you want to build a superb team of sales pros? Do you want an easier job managing and coaching that team? A system makes your life easier because:

1. The best models aren't in the swimsuit issue of *Sports Illustrated.* It's so much more beautiful to model successful sales behavior and achieve similar successful results. Replicate the winners in all the sales personnel in your organization.

2. Your people will learn when to hit the road. A system defines when a sales rep should walk away from a bad prospect. This is huge. You can get your reps to invest and focus time on high-probability prospects.

3. "Show me the money will get easier to say. A proven method makes sure that your reps get critical information during the sales call. This includes budget, decision-makers, time frame to buy, and the true motivation the prospect needs to acquire your product or service.

4. Your reps can close sales with the fast-forward button on. It speeds up the sales cycle. In your mind, you believed this might be true. It *is* true; your team can bring in more business in less time.

5. Whips can be left at home. A system sets standards that supervisory personnel can control and manage. Monitor activity and quantify accurate appraisals of your reps.

6. You won't cuss at your calculator. Performance can be more easily measured. You'll know the closing rates of your reps based on number of leads generated, time invested, how much each rep earns for you, and more.

7. Crystal balls can be left at home. A system is predictable. There'll be very few surprises during the selling process. Your people will always know what's happening next. This eliminates prospects' propensity for hiding behind voicemail!

8. Train derailments are confined to movies. A system keeps salespeople on course during the selling process. As a system manager, you can easily identify where your reps stray and get them back on track.

9. New inventions are confined to television infomercials. Don't reinvent the wheel of sales wisdom. Just implement what already works. That's efficient.

10. Today is *never* the tomorrow you worried about yesterday. Procrastination elimination is in place. Expectations are visible for all to see. There's no question as to the reps' planned activities. Either the reps make the effort or they're gone.

Notice the use of strong terms, like *enforce, mandatory,* and *elimination.* You know you'd like to be tougher on your reps, but fear it would be counter-productive. Let the system be the bad guy! When a rep stumbles, point to the place in the system where the misstep occurred, and help him or her grow as a pro. Use the system to enforce behavior. Your rep has agreed to abide by the system (if he or she wants to play with your team), so there's no confusion about what anyone should be doing at any given moment in their sales life.

So, *Why Aren't You Using A System?* Why aren't you insisting that your company implement one as quickly as possible? How much more money will you leave on the table before you realize that this makes as much sense as any business advice you've ever received?

The last image I want to leave with you is of my fist *pounding* on the desk while I'm typing this statement on the keyboard with one hand:

"WHY AREN'T YOU USING A SYSTEM TO INCREASE SALES?"

JUST A LITTLE REMINDER THAT YOU'RE RESPONSIBLE FOR INCREASING SALES.

SalesAutopsy.com

Appendix A.

Recommended Resources

Books

I'm what you might call a prolific reader. In the twenty-three years since I graduated from college, I've consumed approximately six thousand books. Lately I've been able to "read" more as business books on tape become commonplace. Actually, that number would be higher, but I need to take my three-year-old's penny out of my car's cassette player.

I only buy books that are *extraordinary*. These books are absolutely genius. You should own them.

Sales

The Sales Bible by Jeffrey Gitomer

Power Based Selling by Jim Holden

Let's Get Real or Let's Not Play by Mahan Khalsa

Close the Deal (selling checklists) by Sam Deep & Lyle Sussman

How to Sell Your Way Through Life by Napoleon Hill

The Sales Funnel by Ray Leone

How to Sell Yourself to Others by Kevin Hogan (title not finalized at press time)

How to Become a Rainmaker by Jefferey Fox

Marketing

Triggers by Joseph Sugarman

Magical Worlds of the Wizard of Ads by Roy H. Williams

The Wizard of Ads by Roy H. Williams

Secret Formulas of the Wizard of Ads by Roy H. Williams

101 Ways to Promote Yourself by Raleigh Pinskey

The 22 Immutable Laws of Marketing by Al Ries & Jack Trout

Swim With the Sharks by Harvey MacKay

Cash Copy by Dr. Jeffrey Lant

Marketing Outrageously by Jon Spoelstra (buy it for the cover, too!)

Shameless Marketing for Brazen Hussies by Marilyn Ross

Networking

Masters of Networking by Dr. Ivan Misner

The World's Best Known Marketing Secret by Dr. Ivan Misner

Dig Your Well Before You're Thirsty by Harvey MacKay

Creativity

Serious Creativity by Dr. Edward deBono

Six Thinking Hats (strategizing tool) by Dr. Edward deBono

Thinkertoys by Michael Michalko

Humor

How to Be Funny: Discovering the Comic You by Steve Allen

Jest for Success by Malcolm Kushner

SOHO (Home-based Business)

Getting Business to Come to You by Paul & Sarah Edwards

Working from Home by Paul & Sarah Edwards

Working Solo Series by Terri Lonier

Speaking

Speak and Grow Rich by Dottie Walters and Lilly Walters

The Quick and Easy Way to Effective Speaking
by Dale Carnegie

How to Get Your Point Across in 30 Seconds or Less
by Milo O. Frank

Speaking Secrets of the Masters by Speaker's Roundtable

Tested Public Speaking by Elmer Wheeler

Improving Your Storytelling by Doug Lipman

Free Radio Airtime by Earl Nightengale

Reference (expensive, use the library)

Associations Unlimited (organizations to work with)
by Gale Publications

Bartlett's Directory of Anecdotes (great stories about famous people)

Oxbridge Directory of Newsletters (marketing publications that you never knew about!) by Oxbridge Press

All-in-One Media Directory (where to get free publicity, find journalists, experts, and more) by Gebbie Press

Sales eBook

Make Your Site Sell 2002 by Ken Evoy (www.sitesell.com)

Ezines

Go to my website for an extensive report on the best sales and marketing ezines: www.SalesAutopsy.com/book

Magazines

If you want a single resource to discover magazines that you should read or submit articles to or advertise in, check out this comprehensive website:
www.newsdirectory.com/news/magazine/business/

Testing

Can you evaluate your selling potential? How about the potential of the reps you might need to hire, or of those already in place? There's one company with a testing product that pinpoints each critical improvement area of a salesperson's life. You can determine who can get better and by how much. You can accurately decide whom to hire and whom you should fire (if you've got the guts). Contact Objective Management and receive a free assessment — just for readers of this book. Go to the following Web address:
www.objectivemanagement.com/SalesAssessment.htm.

Free Reports

1. How to find your exact buyer (in large quantities) on the World Wide Web

2. How to identify a quality training organization

3. What are the top marketing ezines on-line?

Go to my website and request these reports.

Salesautopsy.com/book

Free Excuses

If you don't want to change how you sell: You had some good laughs here, but don't want to go through the effort of adopting new strategies. In other words, you're really happy with your abilities, your prospects, and your earnings. I highly recommend you check out Craig Boldan's *Every Excuse in the Book.* Here you can select from alibis like:

My underwear cut off the blood flow to my brain

I'm messed up from reading self-help books

I'll never need this in the real world

I drank milk past the expiration date

I misplaced my moral compass

Free Sales Joke

The purpose of this book is to emphasize that if you get training and really "own" a selling system, your life will be easier. You'll have less stress during your sales life. This true story reinforces that idea that you can worry less about your future:

A huge stretch limousine pulls up in front of the Waldorf Astoria Hotel in New York City. A wealthy woman steps out and asks the doorman to get fourteen bellhops to help her. They line up and she directs each one to grab some luggage and move it into her suite. As the last piece of luggage disappears, one lone bellman is left looking at her.

"Go into the car and pick up my son and carry him inside." The bellman opens the door and sees a thirteen-year-old boy, immensely fat, spread onto the seat like melted butter. He turns to the woman and says, "Can't he just walk to the room himself?"

"Yes, he can," she replies. *"But thank God he'll never have to."*

Free Lunch

THERE IS NO FREE LUNCH!

Appendix B.

Teaching Consequences
to Your Prospects:

*A superb selling secret
for the new millennium*

I'M EXTREMELY HAPPY with my sales abilities today. I feel like I could walk into any selling scenario and help a prospect see his or her exact reasons for buying what I offer. I also know that if I wanted to go back to work for a company (rather than myself), I could land the job I want, anywhere I want to live. Think about that ... Wanna live at the ocean, in the mountains, in another country? Great salespeople have those options.

But I have to confess that my sales life wasn't always like that. When I was forced into being a sales trainer by taking a management role, I decided to read every book on selling, attend every seminar I could find, and talk to successful sales pros to learn their secrets. I've continued to do that over the past fifteen years. In spite of this massive education, you probably recall how I previously painted my old sales life as a series of events where great sales reps would kick sand in my face and take my commissions.

Then I discovered the most effective selling strategy in existence today. You must teach *consequences* to your prospects.

Credit for this concept includes not only all the years I grew from being beaten up in selling, but also to several training organizations that focus on alternatives to feature-benefit selling. They include the Sandler Sales Institute, Franklin Covey Sales Performance group, Provant Solution Selling Program, Huthwaite Group Spin Selling, Sharon Drew Morgan's Selling With Integrity, and several sharp sales pros who know how to dig into a prospect's problems and help them recognize what the real trouble is. In addition, I was delighted to discover that the oldest sales training organization in America - Dale Carnegie Training (which offered their first sales course in 1939), has incorporated this concept into their questioning strategies. Their Sales Advantage program teaches selling professionals to follow a line of inquiry that flows from how things are today to the ultimate effect a solution has upon an organization. Their model is divided into four levels of queries. Read the following four descriptions from bottom to top, just as you would begin a selling relationship from the groundfloor and move to the ceiling of success:

- **Payout** questions reveal the impact a solution offers to the company and individual buyer.

- **Barrier** questions identify factors keeping the buyer from the should be.

- **Should Be** questions help discover the buyer's vision of optimal performance.

- **As Is** questions determine a buyer's current situation.

I've expanded the usefulness of their ideas here by helping you realize the psychology of how consequences work. It is rooted in how we grow up and learn to do decision-making. As a sales professional, entrepreneur, manager, or trainer, it's always helpful to understand the reason why a strategy works. You don't have to accept the concept of consequences on blind faith, you know it's a part of your past. Now you have a frame of reference for the validity of this approach. This will give you the foundation to see how effective this selling strategy is — when you decide to build it into your conversations with prospects.

Let's begin by viewing my sales presentations — before and after I was a ninety-pound weakling rubbing sand out of my eyes.

Before

As a recruiter, it was my job to pitch outstanding candidates to employers looking for salespeople. I attacked the marketplace like hundreds of other recruiters in Chicago. Our collective phone calls, thousands of them each week, all sounded like this:

Dan: Hello (decision-maker), I understand that you're looking for a salesperson, and I would like to share a great one with you. She has hit 150 percent of her quota the past three years, is trained by Xerox, which you know is outstanding, and she has made President's Club — that's top 10 percent — for her firm the past two years. What an excellent addition she'd make to your team. (I was about to get hit with any of a dozen objections.)

Decision-maker: We don't pay fees to headhunters, we require a college degree, she'd need ten years in selling, she hasn't sold in our industry, I already have plenty of candidates from my ad in the paper, it's late in the interviewing process. And if she's doing so well, why is she looking? And so on.

It was the beginning of a verbal arm-wrestling match. Except it didn't matter if my larynx was stronger; the prospect could always just hang up the phone. Selling by pitching this way was exhausting, discouraging, and demeaning. There had to be a better way for my energy and my ego.

After

I'll never forget the first time I used consequences (in fact, when I speak on this experience I get goose bumps recalling it). I created a list of questions that pointed to the impact of the missing sales rep problem (you'll learn how to do this shortly). Here's how the conversation with that first sales manager evolved:

Dan: Hi, John, I heard you had an open territory, how's it going?

John: Well, I'm very busy interviewing people now. (Notice he's setting me up to get off the phone with the "very busy" comment.)

Dan: Good, hope you find someone. So who's covering that open territory?

John: I am.

Dan: In addition to managing your other people and all your other work?

John: Yes.

191

Dan: Oh. no, that's probably not taking too much extra time from your day?

John: No, it's not really affecting my days, I just work into the evening. (He laughed, he's forming rapport with me.)

Dan: Since you've been doing the work of this missing person, is your family okay with the extra hours you're putting in?

(After a long pause)

John: You know what, I haven't been home for dinner in two weeks. And my wife is a great cook! (He said those exact words.)

I continued, asking other consequence questions, like "Do your competitors know that these accounts aren't being visited?" "Is the missing person costing the company much money?" "Is this costing *you* money?" The situation was being framed by the trauma caused by the missing sales rep.

Five minutes into the phone call, he asked me if I had anyone for him to see. Imagine that! I hadn't presented a product or service to him. I hadn't presented any benefits I could offer. There wasn't even a hint that I had a solution for his problem. But he knew one thing about me that was true: I knew his situation, his personal experience, almost as intimately as he did. So who was better qualified to help him — me, or the other pushy parrots calling to "present" candidates for the job?

Proof

I later had a unique experience when that potential client (who became a buyer and a friend) told me what happened after we had that discussion on the consequences of his decision making. He said our conversation was so unusual that he told his wife about it at home that evening (after eating leftovers). He told her that while the choices between my service and a competitor's were fairly even, I had a *much* better understanding of the *complete reality, the scope,* of the decision. And that's why he chose to do business with me.

Workshop for Winning

Teaching Consequences to Prospects

SOME OF WHAT YOU'RE ABOUT TO READ would be considered controversial. It flies in the face of mainstream selling practices. Stick with me here. If what you're presently doing works well (makes plenty of money!), that's great. If what you're about to learn here is useful or better, you'll be pleased that you were open to adopting a new strategy.

During speaking engagements, I often hint at the thought that feature-and-benefit selling is no longer the most effective sales approach. If there were tomatoes in the room, I'd probably end up wearing them.

Here's a question for you: Do prospects buy for your reasons or their own? The answer is obvious, of course — people buy for their own reasons. In fact that question is so simple, you might be insulted that I asked it of you. But if people really do have their own grounds for choosing to acquire a product or service, *why do we insist on forcing our reasons upon them?* We do it all the time when we use features and benefits to sell. When we whip out that laundry list of all the great things that will happen when people buy from us, we're betting that one of those items will strike a chord and motivate a prospect to become a client. Think this through and decide whether this bet is really worth putting your income, career, and family life on the line for.

If you hadn't noticed, feature-benefit selling is dying. Like Elvis, it might possibly be dead. Feature benefit selling began to get old and gray in the '90s. The biggest problem I have with this approach is that it makes all salespeople sound alike. And remember that we revealed earlier the value of uniqueness in selling. Features and benefits are about the salesperson's perception of what's important to the prospect. They have little to do with the prospect's reality. Ninety percent of the salespeople out there are unbearably ordinary. You want to keep away from these dangerous depths of mediocrity.

We're not letting you marketing people off the hook, either (and

193

you entrepreneurs who create your own literature). If you're designing brochures in print or on-line, you still need to address the issue of whether you're pushing what you "think" is important to potential buyers. If you're guessing that your list of benefits might strike home and turn a prospect into a buyer, I have further news — you're not selling, you're hoping.

There is a way to sell effectively and uniquely today — if setting you apart from and ahead of the competition matters. You must learn to teach *consequences* to your prospects.

Here's a revelation for you: You know all about consequences already, and I'm going to show you how you do.

Remember when you were a little guy or girl and adults had to teach you things like don't touch a hot stove, and look both ways before crossing the street? The adults would conclude their warning with a consequence: "you'll burn your hand" or, "you'll get hit by a car." This was meant to etch into your brain the seriousness of your mistake. You want to use similar language that nurtures your prospects while warning them of danger. You're going to play the adult to your child/prospect. You can learn to engage in discussions that will prevent your prospects from burning their butts on the job or getting run over by the competition.

How does that conversation work?

Your agenda on a sales call will be to help your buyer discuss *and take ownership of* the company and the individual negative impact of the way he or she does business *without or until* the time he or she acquires and implements your product or service. Briefly, you'll discuss how and when they're going to get their butts burned — until the problem is solved.

How does this work better than feature-benefit selling? Back to why people buy — for your reasons or theirs? Would it be fair to say that few prospects trust us until they see that we understand their situation? When we can define a prospect's personal problems (that we can solve), then show empathy or understanding of those troubles, trust begins to evolve. Notice that we're ultimately referring to *personal* problems, not company problems. Company problems might be the reason you got your appointment, your foot in the door. Now you need to be able to take a comfortable seat to discuss consequences if you plan on a long, strong relationship. You need to realize how these company problems have a personal impact on your buyer. This personal impact is the focus of your conversations on the sales call.

Here's how I look at the use of consequences from the buyer's point of view: He or she is going to write the sequel to his current tale of trouble. Essentially, that buyer can choose the ending to his or her story. You will help them script that conclusion.

Getting to this on a personal level during the sales process takes some time, rapport, and good questions. You need to invest the time and show concern for the prospect's situation in order to generate true rapport. That's the point at which you can say almost anything and get away with it. You know what I mean, too. Think of all the times that you wanted to say something out of anger, frustration, or wonderment at the sheer stupidity of the buyer, when they just don't get it! Ninety-eight percent of the time, you don't dare open your mouth. When in rapport with them, you're going to be amazed at what you can get away with saying. It's identical to getting in the face of a friend when you disagree with his or her opinion. Because respect and some relational history exists, you can share how you feel — without placing your buyer/seller relationship on the endangered species list.

Proof

To further reinforce the usefulness of this selling strategy, I'll share another experience I had with Denise, who is a classic rags-to-riches story, having moved from a secretarial position to CEO of her own promotions firm. Because of her path to the top, she'd never had the chance to get a selling system under her belt. I made two calls on her to get her into a two-year training program that would further change her life. The second call was to pick up the check for her commitment to the class. As you probably do, I attempted to discover what might unsell her or cause buyer's remorse. I asked, "Denise, what's the real reason you want to do this training? I mean, two years is a serious commitment."

Her answer was a total surprise and still gives me chills when I replay it in my mind. "I want to be able to do exactly what you did to me. I don't know what you did, but I want to know how to do it.

How did you sell me?" It was my ultimate compliment as a sales professional and a trainer.

So, when the prospect goes back to review his or her choices on which salesperson to work with, which sales pro understands the buyer's situation, the buyer's vulnerability, the best? You, the seller motivating the buyer with consequences!

Here are some insights on teaching consequences to your prospects:

1. You do a lot less talking.

2. You don't have to be able to "handle objections" since you offer nothing to object to.

3. You know what the real trouble is — it's not a missing salesperson. It's all the aggravation — corporate, financial, and most of all personal — to the person dealing with the problems that can be fixed with your product or service.

Here are some insights on using feature-and-benefit selling:

1. You play the numbers game, so luck (or cherry-picking for good prospects), becomes an important part of your income.

2. You sell on price, so your best potential earnings are often at risk.

3. You sound like every other salesperson out there, so you're not memorable.

One of the strange things about using consequences is that the buyer doesn't know what strategy is being used. He or she gets caught up in the concerns being discussed. On the other hand, in a feature-and-benefit presentation, the buyer is painfully aware of what you're trying to pull because it's what the buyer always experiences with salespeople.

Let's look at another scenario using the consequence process. This is a snapshot of my conversation with a buyer. It takes guts, but it shows them that you're on track with their situation (remember, I only do this after we're both comfortable with each other):

Dan: Well, you have a difficult decision, trying to choose the right company to service you. But if you chose the wrong company, that probably wouldn't be that big of a deal?

Buyer: Well, it could show my boss that I don't make the best decisions.

Dan: So, that's probably not good for you in the long run? But you've been here a long time; you'd be okay if you made the wrong choice.

Buyer: Not necessarily. My raise or a promotion might be at risk if I made a couple of bad choices.

Dan: Really? It's that serious?

Buyer: It is. And I don't take risks making business decisions where my career is a factor.

Dan: That certainly makes sense to me. You've got to make the best call for your company. But if you chose wrong in a big decision, you wouldn't get fired, would you?

Now how's that for personal consequences? We moved from the boss' concerns about decision making (not good), to missing a promotion (pretty bad), to losing one's job (infinitely worse).

Let's get into the actual steps for developing the language you need for teaching consequences to your prospects.

The Workshop

The best way to equip you with the most effective language to use with prospects is to begin with the traditional feature-benefit approach. Most organizations already have literature that was designed based on benefits. This will provide us with a launching pad that we'll move away from as we use selling words that propel us — and our earnings — sky-high.

I'll use a basic example, automobile sales, to get you comfortable with this practice of altering words in print and in person. Remember, I said I wasn't letting the marketing people off the hook? You'll want to consider the use of this language for your lead-generating literature as well.

(The Way of the Dinosaur)

Five Reasons to Buy A Car Today

- Prestige of owning a new car
- Cool color
- 0–60 mph in eight seconds
- Rides and handles like a dream
- 100-year warranty

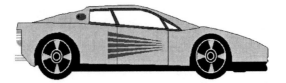

(The Way of the New Millennium)

Features & Benefits	Consequences
Five Reasons to Buy a Car Today (Seller)	**Five Reasons to Buy Today (Buyer)**
• Prestige of owning a new car	• Can't take a client to lunch in my car
• Cool color	• Old look says that I'm not successful
• 0–60 mph in eight seconds	• Dangerous to merge in traffic
• Rides and handles like a dream	• I feel every bump in the road
• 100-year warranty	• Surprised by what breaks down every month

Learn to Sell Right!

That is, sell on the *right side* of this page.

Here's a sample list of consequences you'll be looking for:

Corporate

- Irrecoverable or squandered revenue, market share, or market-place status
- Fear about the company's future
- Angry shareholders
- Embarrassment to customers
- Sending a bad or wrong message to customers and/or employees
- Mistrust of a company's offerings and products

Individual

- Ruined advancement opportunity or obstruction of career path
- Reduced or lost income potential
- Loss of personal prestige
- Corporate doubt about abilities
- Inefficient work processes that increase workload and steal time from family
- Wasted efforts to close business or build business
- Family frustration over work issues

Sit down and begin to design questions that stir up this pot of consequences. You'll want to ask the prospect for his or her initial feelings about what the trouble is, then say things like, "So, does this also mean … consequence?" or "Wow, who's going to deal with … consequence?" or "That's not good if … consequence."

Remember: You want to begin with the company consequences, then move to the personal.

These steps form your path to closing more business. Learn to walk your prospect down this trail and you'll have conversations you've never before experienced in selling. You'll gather rich information that will help you gather more riches for you and your family.

If you'd prefer to have me come to your company and work through this whole process, building powerful language that will distinguish you from the competition and make your selling life more fruitful, call or email Dan Seidman: 847-359-7860 or dan@SalesAutopsy.com

Good Hunting!

Index

W

Z

CONFESS...

Your Worst, Your Most Embarrassing Sales Experience

READING THESE STORIES probably reminded you of some of your not-so-memorable sales memories. I'd love to hear from you.

Share your tale:

If it ends up in my next book, *you'll win* a copy!

If it shows up in our newsletter, ***you'll win the current prize*** offered at our **www.SalesAutopsy.com** website!

There are four ways to *confess*:

1. You can email your story to
   warstory@SalesAutopsy.com

2. You can fax your story to 801-881-8316

3. You can submit your story at the
   www.SalesAutopsy.com website!

4. You can mail it to Sales Autopsy Press, 190 E. Dundee Rd., Barrington, IL 60010

Thank you!

Dan Seidman